Taking Control

Mary Helen Ponce

Arte Publico Press
Houston

a grant from the National
agency.

Cover art by: Manuel Neri, Untitled V, 1985 mixed media on paper, 49 1/2 x 29 3/4 inches, Thomas M. and Joanna S. Hirst Collection.

Back cover photo by: Jerry Clark

Arte Publico Press
University of Houston
Houston, Texas 77004

ISBN 0-934770-70-0
LC 87-070272
Copyright © 1987 by Mary Helen Ponce
Printed in the United States of America

Contents

The Playgoers

The Playgoers

The lights went out just as Doña Fedelia found a seat in the front row of the dimly lit theatre. For a minute she could not see. Only the bulky figure of her friend and neighbor, Doña Adelaida, appeared familiar. Doña Fedelia blinked, trying to adjust to the dark, then her eyes focused on a red light that appeared near center stage. She groped in her purse for her bifocals, then put them on, adjusted the wire frames around her small ears and sat down before the play began.

Doña Fedelia felt suddenly tired. She preferred to be at home in her rocking chair crocheting and watching the Spanish-language station. But Becky, her daughter, had been insistent, demanding she attend this play.

"Ay, Mama, you have to get out and do things."

"Out?"

"Si. Go with me to see a play."

"And what do I want with a play? I'm happy just staying at home."

"Ay, Mama. Just try it. Invite Doña Ada. Come on! There's nothing wrong with plays. You'll like it. Be a play-goer, come on."

"Bueno pues, just this one time."

Tired of making excuses for not wanting to attend movies or lunch with her daughter, Doña Fedelia finally gave in. At times she felt guilty about liking her own company best. However, once she gave Becky her word, she reluctantly went next door to invite Doña Ada who immediately went indoors to get ready. They then waited for Becky in Doña Fedelia's living room. As they waited they talked of inconsequential things: the new postman, the price of eggs, their former neighbor Don Pedro, who was recently buried at nearby Evergreen Cemetery, and his widow Doña Marta, who had

6

worn black for only two weeks! They were nearly asleep—Doña Fedelia's head slumping down onto her chest, Doña Ada snoring softly—when Becky dashed in, rushed them into her VW bug and took them off to the Playgoers, to el teatro.

"And what are we going to see?" asked Doña Fedelia, adjusting the string of yellow pearls that hung on her ample chest. "¿Es en español?"

"No. There's several plays, mama. The one we're going to see is a classic. I think it's called "The Moon Only Shines for a Fool." The guy who wrote it won some prize. It's supposed to take place in Spain."

"I like it already," chortled Doña Adelaida in anticipation.

"I'm only going because you insist," piped in Doña Fedelia.

"... And it better not be vulgar . . ."

"Ay, Mama. This is a musical. You'll like it. It's fun to go to plays." Becky smiled into the front mirror, then made a swift turn from Santa Monica Boulevard onto the freeway. "I went to a lot of trouble to get the tickets, Mama. So please try to . . ."

"Ay, watch out you don't kill us," squealed Doña Fedelia. "¡Jesus, Maria y Jose! You drive like a crazy woman. That's why your car is such a mess."

"Mess? This car is a classic."

"Ummm. Maybe, but it's too small. We're packed in like sardines."

"I have plenty of room," offered Doña Adelaida from the back seat. "I like small cars, especially convertibles."

"Huh! You should be so young," smirked Doña Fedelia, turning up her nose. "Face it, we're just two old crows."

Becky swiftly turned on the radio, aware the two women were about to begin the never-ending argument on age. Old age. She eased the car into a parking lot, found a small opening between two cars and then helped the women out. They walked toward the window in the old building that said Box

Office and looked around. Doña Fedelia was about to comment that the building didn't resemble a theatre, but held back. She was determined to have a good time, which meant she should keep her opinions to herself. She smiled while Becky fished in her purse for the theatre tickets.

"Dammit. I had them right here," hissed Becky, rummaging through her purse; anxious to take the women inside. A small crowd had gathered; Doña Fedelia was starting to turn up her nose at other playgoers, especially at the women with blue and purple hair. Doña Ada, however, smiled at everyone, including a couple dressed completely in black, with chains on their arms, their short, short hair sticking out. Finally Becky found the tickets, then guided the women up a rickety set of stairs. She stopped twice to allow them to catch their breath. They ascended to a lobby adjacent to three doors, each with a sign that read Theatre I, Theatre II, Theatre III. Becky told the women to wait while she went off to find an usher. She wanted to make sure they entered the right door, found the right play. She had just turned the corner when an usher appeared from inside Theatre I and in a curt tongue suggested to the two elderly women that they find their seats. Not knowing what else to do, the embarrassed women turned toward the door of Theatre II.

Doña Fedelia stood next to Doña Ada in the darkened lobby, shifting her tired feet, determined not to complain. She thought of her comfortable chair at home and the soap opera she was missing. "I should have stayed home," she grumbled, clutching her purse to her chest. Just then Doña Ada nudged her toward the middle door saying, "Let's go in." Doña Fedelia followed, muttering under her breath. They were groping their way down the dark aisle when the usher appeared and hissed, "This way please," and shoved them into two seats in the front row.

When Becky returned to the foyer, she almost panicked at not seeing the two ladies. They must have gone to the bathroom, she reasoned. So she skipped down the stairs once more. She was dismayed to find the bathroom empty. She dashed up the stairs again, panting and gasping for air, and ran out to the front entrance shouting, "Mama, Doña Ada!" Just then she saw the usher coming toward her.

"I'm sorry, miss," he intoned, "you'll have to take your seat. The play is about to begin."

"But I've lost my mother!"

"No one gets lost here, miss. Better find your seat; there's few left." He then disappeared down the stairs.

Becky stood against the wall, staring at the three doors. Dammit. Which of the three doors could they have entered? *Shit*. It will take me forever to find them in the dark. I'll just have to wait till intermission, she finally decided, as around her other playgoers scurried to find a seat. She continued to wait a bit more, but then took a deep breath, looked around once and walked into Theatre III.

When the music began Doña Fedelia quickly raised her hands to her ears, then remembering where she was, clasped them in her ample lap. She snorted aloud, her lined lips pursed in a disapproving frown. This looked like a low-class place! On stage actors were moving about to the beat of the music that blared from a corner speaker. They twirled and gyrated, their shiny, sinuous bodies coming closer. Doña Fedelia quickly adjusted her bifocals and looked up. Few of the dancers were wearing clothes! ¡*Dios mio*! The women wore skimpy tops; their legs were encased in sparkling tights. The men too wore tights. Tight, tight tights! As they came near, Doña Fedelia's eyes glazed over. The men wore nothing underneath! She could make out the outline of their firm, round bodies. Jesus, Maria y Jose, she sighed, breaking out in a sweat. This must be a strip tease joint. She closed her eyes and sank back against the seat, prepared for the worst.

Doña Adelaida was having a good time. As the music blared, she tapped her foot on the rough cement floor; her fingers marked time on the armrest: tap, tap, tap. She smiled at the dancers, striving to remember if this music was known as the blues or jazz. She smiled at the men and women in shiny, bright leotards. They looked happy and healthy, she thought. And so very young! She could smell their sweating bodies, but did not find this unpleasant. She inhaled deeply, her swollen feet keeping time to the music. She felt happy. Music and people made her happy. She craned her neck to see the men dancing on stage. Next to them stood a short, dark man playing a saxophone. Now she knew the music was jazz! Elated, she turned around to Doña Fedelia to be met with a dark, disapproving glare.

Inside Theatre III Becky sat furiously chewing gum, twisting the straps of her purse. She had picked up the tickets during her lunch hour and was now starving . . . and furious. She was angry at herself for not giving her mother and Doña Ada explicit directions. Darn! She so badly wanted to please her mother, and now this! She craned her neck to look for them once more, but the theatre was too dark. In anger and frustration she settled back to watch the unfolding play.

On the stage two figures appeared. Becky sat up in her seat. It was Don Quixote and Sancho Panza! This Spanish classic tale was one of her mother's favorite. She finally sat back. All eyes were riveted on the two men on stage who appeared to be preparing for a trip. The other plays can't possibly compare with this, thought Becky. She closed her eyes, leaned back into the lumpy seat and felt herself carried away to another time, another place. Don Quixote was whispering words of love to a lovely damsel, love words Becky knew were no longer in vogue: *Querida, amada mia, mi amor*. Becky felt her skin crawl. She forgot all about having lost her mother, determined to at least enjoy the first act.

The first time the male dancer in purple tights came close, Doña Fedelia instinctively pulled in her feet. How dare he, she thought. If he so much as touches me, I'll scream! She cleared her throat in warning, but Doña Ada, lost in the music, ignored her. Doña Fedelia had heard about places like this! She knew that men often preyed on older women and forced them to do terrible things, things too terrible to even think of. Then they left them to die in some dark alley. She reached inside her plump purse for the mace canister Becky had given her. If he so much as touches me, she swore, *lo mato*, I'll kill him. She took a deep breath, crossed her tired feet and glanced at Doña Ada who was perspiring freely; a small fan in her hand moved slowly back and forth.

Doña Ada liked to think she possessed a "cosmopolitan flair." She usually carried a black silk fan and white linen handkerchief in her purse. Most of her clothes were bought at the Goodwill or other thrift shops she frequented. She still clung to the fashions of her era, the 1940s, and was delighted when draped dresses with wide shoulder pads were once more in vogue. More than this, Doña Ada wore hats with a veil. She still had most of her favorites, such as the one she wore: a small satin hat with rhinestone clips on each side and at the crown and a veil dotted with shiny sequins. Doña Ada *knew* she looked "smart," except for her sensible black shoes which were prescribed by her podiatrist. She smiled at Doña Fedelia—who was ignoring her—and at the elderly man who sat next to her and who now and then pressed his foot against hers.

Becky sat enthralled as on stage Don Quixote leaned against a Spanish wall covered in honeysuckle, reciting poems to his sweetheart who was standing with her duenna. From her seat Becky made out the soft words of love. Tears stung her eyes. Oh for love like this! For words like these! And for a world of real men. Strong, loving men, not like the jerks she worked with at Northwest Telephone, all of whom were out for one thing only. Few of them read the classics or liked plays. None had expressed an interest in the discount tickets offered. Only Becky. She had heard that some of the plays were quite risque, especially one full of New York actors who appeared almost in the nude and did nasty things while on stage. Clearly, thought Becky, none could compare with Don Quixote. If only she could find her mother and Doña Adelaida, everything would be perfect.

In the front row of Theatre II Doña Fedelia sat rigid against the seat. Twice the male dancer in purple tights had ventured near, too near, then moved on to shake his behind at a young woman with spiked hair who was sitting near the aisle. Doña Fedelia relaxed her hold on the mace; perhaps she might not need it after all! The bright lights shone on a man and woman on stage who were kissing and fondling each other. The half-dressed woman climbed into the bed as the man—in a white suit similar to that worn by Gilbert Roland, the movie star of the '40s—began to take off his clothes.

When the man on stage began unzipping his pants, Doña Fedelia reached into her purse for a kleenex to clean her sweating brow. Aghast at the scenario taking place on the dimly lit stage, she was determined not to make a spectacle of herself. She looked up once more at the stage, then brought the tissue to her face. The man had removed all his clothes! His back was to the audience. Doña Fedelia could plainly see his behind gleaming in the soft light. *Jesus, Maria y Jose*, she thought, her heart thumping furiously. Her breathing grew labored; she knew she would faint. How dare Becky do this to her? She made as if to stand, but just then the male dancer in the purple tights moved in. She quickly unzipped her purse and felt for the mace.

When first she felt the pressure on her foot, Doña Adelaida ignored it. When this continued, she turned around, an apology on her lips. Perhaps, she thought, I am tapping my feet too loud! She turned and discovered an elderly man next to her. A handsome old-timer beamed at her from behind thick glasses. His moon face appeared pleasant; white wisps of hair fell across his brow. "Excuse me," he murmured. "Oh, it was my fault," gushed Doña Ada. She quickly moved her hat veil aside, the better to see him. "It was my fault," she insisted, smiling coyly from behind the veil, her eyes riveted on his moon face. She then remembered having read that a veil will convey an aura of mystery. She quickly pulled it down. Once more she smiled at the elderly man from behind the sequins, then she returned her attention to the stage where a tall, handsome man in a white suit was taking off his pants.

As the first act continued, Becky sat in a trance. The melodious strings of the Spanish guitars had lulled her. Don Quixote, dressed in shining armor, walked toward his horse; behind him trudged the portly Sancho Panza; to the side stood Dulcinea del Toboso. Once again the guitarist played a love song. Becky squirmed in her seat, thinking of her former boyfriend Eddie, and of the night they broke off their engagement. She could still recall how distraught she felt as they stood outside El Pollo Loco on 3rd and Soto, and how she cried clinging to Eddie saying, "We can work it out, Eddie. We can." But Eddie had pushed her from him saying, "Later." God, thought Becky, her moist eyes riveted on the armor-clad figure, why wasn't Eddie more like Don Quixote? Why didn't he at least cry . . . or recite a poem? All Eddie had said was, "later," as he climbed into his red Camaro and drove off into the night. Becky thought her heart would break, as Don Quixote knelt at Dulcinea's feet to profess undying love. Oh God, she sighed, where is the romance? Where is love? She snuggled deep into the seat, as tears rolled down her cheeks.

Doña Fedelia could feel her eyes watering and her heart thumping. On stage the naked man got into the bed where the woman awaited him. Now they were both under the covers! Doña Fedelia tried not to look. She held the program to her face and ashamedly glanced around. All eyes were focused on the couple. When next she looked, Doña Fe saw only the woman's face. Where is the man, she wondered? She was about to ask Doña Ada when she saw that the bedcovers were moving. Suddenly she felt nauseous. She knew she would faint. Just then the music began; the dancers moved around the darkened stage. Doña Fedelia, her hand steady on the mace canister, braced herself.

In Theatre III all was silent. Don Quixote knelt to receive the blessing of the bishop, as offstage a choir sang a *Te Deum*. This act sure is long, mumbled Becky, reaching for the program. She flipped through it, then sat up. *Damm!* These were one-act plays! Jesus H. Christ! My mama won't get to see this! Becky felt contrite, knowing that somewhere in the building her mother was stuck watching a boring play. She surveyed the crowd once more, hoping to spot her mother as on stage, Don Quixote, his lance by his side, sang an adieu.

"Adelaida, Adelaida," Doña Fedelia gasped. "I'm going to die." She yanked at Doña Ada's dress sleeve, certain that she was having a heart attack. All the known symptoms were present: blurred vision, shortness of breath and palpitations of the heart.

"Psss, Ada." Doña Fedelia persisted, determined to catch her friend's attention, but Doña Ada, deep in conversation with an elderly gentleman, refused to turn around. Doña Fedelia then did as her doctor recommended: she took a deep breath, then several more until she felt her heart return to normal and her eyes able to focus. Only then did she dare look toward the stage, at nudies who by now were out of the bed and fully dressed. Doña Fedelia sighed in relief, as the couple embraced, then drifted towards the wings. Once more the dancers moved in with precise, expert movements.

Inside Theatre III Becky once more wiped her eyes. The play was finally over. Don Quixote and Sancho Panza faded into the sunset as the curtains came down to loud applause. Becky quickly shoved her way to the lobby where she surveyed the elderly. "Old fogey's," Becky thought smiling, no longer upset. Don Quixote's message of love had melted her heart. She was certain that within minutes her mother and Doña Ada would surge through the crowd. She leaned against the lobby wall, fished in her purse for a cigarette, lit it and inhaled deeply, unaware of a small group of people holding up an elderly woman who was now moving toward her.

When she spotted Becky in the theatre lobby, Doña Fedelia knew she was saved. She would not die among those shameless pigs. She waved a feeble hand at Becky, straining to get her attention. She felt faint, but inhaled, took a firm step buoyed up by the janitor and Doña Adelaida's new-found friend. She felt exhausted; her heart thumped furiously, as sweat glistened on her wrinkled brow. Her bifocals clung tenaciously to her nose.

Becky looked up, gave a startled cry and rushed toward her mother.

"Ay, Mama! What happened?"

"Uhh. Ay, ay," Doña Fedelia clutched at Becky. "Take me home, hija, I can't take any more."

Visibly alarmed, Becky took her mother's sweaty hand, smiled her appreciation to Doña Ada's new friend and then guided her mother down the stairs and to the exit where they bumped into the smiling usher who said to Becky, "Didn't I tell you they would be okay?"

"Yeah. Uh, thanks."

They half-carried Doña Fedelia to the car. Becky was petrified. What had caused her mother to faint? She was aware that other playgoers were watching the small cortege that now included two punkers with purple hair. "What happened, Mama?" she whispered. "Shall I call an ambulance?"

At the mention of an ambulance Doña Fedelia's head shot up. "No, no. Ay, no." She pressed Becky's hand as if to reassure her, then once more moved forward.

Becky, her face pale, was in a panic. I had no right to make her see a play, she thought. What if she's seriously ill? They shuffled toward the dark parking lot and the few remaining cars. Once inside the small, dusty car, her mother laid back against the seat and shut her eyes tight. In the dim street light her lined face appeared yellow, strained. Only the intelligent eyes that now and then opened belied her condition. Sick at heart, Becky scanned the parking lot for Doña Adelaida who had suddenly disappeared with the elderly man in tow. She spotted them walking toward her, engaged in deep conversation.

"Are we going now?" Doña Ada's eyes, behind the sequined veil shone brightly. In her hand the silk fan fluttered back and forth.

Making an effort to control her agitation, Becky pulled open the car door. Just then Doña Ada stopped to scribble something on a piece of perfumed paper (kept in her purse for such emergencies), handed it to the old man, pushed the seat forward, pulled up her dress and climbed in. Well, thought Becky, adjusting her seat belt, whatever it was that upset my mother sure didn't affect her! She turned on the ignition, put the car in gear and slowly backed out. Once on the freeway, she floored the gas pedal, determined to get home fast.

They passed every car on the road. Now and then Becky looked through the mirror at the two elderly women in the back seat. At the playgoers. One sat slumped across the seat, her face a sickly grey, her eyes shut tight, her mouth wide open. Next to her, the other woman wearing a sequined veil, smiled at the world, as she tapped her fingers to the beat of the jazz that poured from the car radio.

The Campout

The Campout

"Well, Ab, I guess that's it. Everything's in the camper and . . ."

"Daddy, Carlos is sitting on my side!"

"I got here first."

"No, I did. Daddy, make him move!"

"Carlos! Move it. Now! Your sister was there first. I saw her through the car window and . . ."

"Awwww. That's not fair."

"Come on. It's late. The Johnsons are waiting for us. Hey Ab! Bring the thermos, okay?"

"It's under the seat, David."

"Okay, let's see. The doors and windows are locked, the sticks are in place, dogs in back, cat's out, stove out, mail stopped, paper . . . Shit. The heater's still on. I thought I'd turned it off, Ab."

"I'll do it. You check the garage door and . . . Oops! I forgot the fruits and vegetables. They're still in the fridge. Dammit, we'll have to move everything around . . . or buy some in Baja."

"No way Ab. I'm not gonna take a chance on getting something."

"Daddy, Carlos still won't move! Look at him, he's gonna hit me!"

"Carlos!"

"Oh, all right, Dad, but on the way back I'm gonna sit next to the window."

"Ready Ab?"

"Yup, all except for my paints and easel."

"Oh, that."

"What do you mean: that? You've got your beer and fishing stuff, David. Why shouldn't I take my easel?"

"It's a waste of space. We could pack something else . . ."

"Oh, like what? More beer?"

"Hey, folks, Bitsey and I thought you'd gone and left us, huh, sugah?"

"Yeah."

"We're just about ready, ain't we, sugah?"

"Yeah."

"Just gotta check my wallet. Make sure ah gots enough dollars. Heh, heh. Gotta leave room for them pesos. Yessiree, just heard the're paying 200 to 1, that so David?"

"I heard it too."

"You sure do pick the right time to go to Mexico, David."

"Baja."

"No, Mexico. Shit, once we get across that there fence . . ."

"Bridge."

"Bridge. I'm gonna filler-up cheap, buy me some leather boots and two bottles of tequila for uhhh, say ten American dollars?"

"We've got to get there first, Biff."

"Why sure, David, you all just . . ."

"Daddy, I gotta go to the bathroom, and . . ."

"Wait, Stacey. I still gotta get ice. Try to wait, okay, baby?"

"Okay, Daddy."

"Ready, you all?"

"Yeah. Just follow me to the gas station and . . ."

"You betcha. Just lead on 'hombre.' Just lead on!"

"Mommy, are we almost to the bad part?"

"What bad part, Stacey? We haven't even left. What bad part?"

"She means where all those shacks are, where it smells. It's called Ti something."

"Oh, now I understand, Carlos. She means Tijuana. It's really short for tia Juana . . . I think."

"It's so yuckey."

"The people are poor, *m'ija*. There are no jobs, few opportunities. They're doing the best they can."

"Are we poor, Mommy?"

"Well, Stacey, we're not rich. Uhh, your dad works hard and I . . ."

"We're not like them, are we, Daddy?"

"Of course not, Stacey! What a thing to say. They're ummmm, ah Mexicans and . . ."

"Yeah, they're Mexicans."

"So are we, stupid."

"No, I'm not. Daddy, Carlos called me stupid and he says I'm a Mexican too . . ."

"*M'ija*, we are all Mexicanos. But some of us were born in the United States. We're really both, Mexican and Americans, and . . ."

"No way, Ab. No way are my kids going to grow up with that hang-up."

"The truth is not a hang-up, David. I want my kids to feel comfortable with, uhhhh, knowing that . . ."

"Knowing what? Shit, Abby, ever since you took those damn classes, that Chicano Communist stuff, all you talk about is . . ."

"Daddy said shit!"

"Yeah, but he doesn't want *us* to say it!"

"How come, Carlos?"

"Cause it's only for grown-ups."

"I can say it too. Wanna hear me?"

20

"Shhhh."

"Shit. Shit! See?"

"Stacey! Don't use that word. It's not nice!"

"Well, don't you use it, David. Remember, kids learn by example."

"Oh! And is that something you learned in college, Mrs. Professor?"

"No David. I'm only saying . . . Oh, forget it."

"I won't forget it. You think you know everything, but I tell you, you don't. I know what to say in front of my kids, I know . . ."

"Dad, you just passed the gas station."

"Shit."

"Buenas tardes, ¿a donde señores?"

"Vamos a San Quintin, Sir, uhhhh, señor."

"¿Que llevan?"

"Nomas, uhhhh. Abby, how do I say camping gear?"

"Vamos a San Quintin, señores, a encampar. Llevamos solo nuestra comida, ropa, lo necesario."

"Bueno, pasen."

"Uhhh, Sir, señor. La familia atras es con nosotros."

"Yo los veo solos."

"Señor, mi esposo quiere decir que la familia detras viene con nosotros. Somos amigos."

"Si, pues, entendido. Pasen."

"Daddy, I'm scared."

"Shhh, Stacey, they have to stop everyone. It's part of their job."

"Okay, Mommy."

"Mommy, why are there so many people in cars?"

"Because Tijuana is a big city. A lot of people come here to . . ."

"Cross over."

"Where Carlos? Where do they cross over?"

"They swim across, stupid."

"In a swimming pool?"

"No dummy, they swim across over there, see . . ."

"Oh!"

"God, it only gets worse."

"What do you expect, David? People move here to make a better life."

"Yeah, but it sure looks bad. All those shacks. God!"

"Poverty is never pretty, David. They even lack drinking water!"

"Mommie, close your window. It smells yuckey."

"Oh, come on, Stacey. It's not so bad. Hold your nose."

"What are you looking at, Carlos?"

"Some kids over there. The boy with the ice-cream cart and torn pants . . . He looks my age. Almost."

"Oh!"

"Ummmm, at last. Now I can paint to my hearts content, and . . ."

"Gotta unpack first, Ab."

"Yes, but for now let me just breathe the sea air. Ummmm."

"Nice, isn't it?"

"Yes. I'm really glad we came. Oh, hi, Biff!"

"Ahhhhh. Uhhhh. That ocean breeze. Bitsey honey, you all gonna get us a beer?"

"Yeah."

"Gonna set up your tent now, David?"

"As soon as I clean up a space."

"Sure a lot of crap around here!"

"Yeah. Nobody cleans up when they leave. Look at that: cans, bottles, garbage. All kinds of . . ."

"No . . . shit!"

"That too. People empty their holding tanks any old place. They just don't care."

"People around here have holding tanks?"

"No. Campers from home. You know, Americans. Uhhh, *us*."

"Damn gringos."

"Yeah. Well, Biff, gotta get started. Pass the shovel, will you?"

"What a lot of shit!"

"Yeah."

"Damn gringos."

"Yeah, yeah."

"Sleep good, Abby?"

"No, Bitsey, too tired and worn, I guess. And you?"

"Honey, with all that traffic? I mean, who can sleep? Did you all hear them cars out on the beach? I mean, cruising at three in the morning? God! I thought they'd never leave!"

"The cars and the noise were the people clamming. They wait until the tide is out. Whole families work, they also work as a collective, then sell the clams in town. It's their livelihood."

"God-Almighty! Ah thought they was partying . . . all that racket!"

"No, hardly. They'll be back later when the tide's out again."

"Oh look, Ab! There they are now! Look at that, all them kiddies. God! Must be a million. And look. Oh my! That one's pregnant! As big as all get-out. And she's going in the ocean! God-Almighty! Biff, Biff. Honey, you all come here and bring my camera. I gotta get me a picture. For sure I'll never see this at home. Biff, come on, honey, hurry! Did you evah? Did you . . . Abby, where you going? Don't you wanna stay and watch the show?"

"I've already seen this."

"Well honey, if you all want, I won't take no pictures."

"Don't."

"What? And not let the folks at home see what Mexico is like? Why honey, this *is* the good stuff. Say Abby, Abby, come back, will ya?"

"Hurry, Mommie. We're going to the store and Daddy says you're holding us up. What's that you're painting?"

"Some children clamming. They came by while you were gone. I gave them some of your old clothes and cookies, then painted their picture."

"Why do they look sad?"

"Because they're hungry and cold."

"Oh? Are they poor!"

"Yes, they are, but nice. And courteous. I enjoyed painting them. All right, all right, David. I'm coming!"

24

"Nice little town, David. San Quetann, is it?"

"Quintin, Biff. It has quite a history, and has an interesting old English settlement and cemetery, what's more . . ."

"Yeah? Well, let's don't forget to stop at the liquor store, ha, ha. Gotta get me some tequila, Kahlua, gin. Uhh, let's see. I should be able to get it all for uhhh, twenty dollars?"

"God-Almighty! Eggs are a dollar a dozen and tortillas are too!"

"Gas sure is cheap, though, Bitsey. Gotta filler up! Yessiree! Hey, muchacho, filler up. Uhhh, mucho, macho. Mas, mas."

"Biff, honey, gimme some dollars. Ah gotta get me some of that perfume. Ummmm."

"Let's get out of here David. I feel sick."

"Hang on a minute, will you, Ab?"

"I'll try."

"That was a good meal, Abby. How did you fix them clams?"

"Martina taught me. It's called a *"guiso."*

"You all really friends with them people?"

"Yup. Known them five years."

"She the one with thirteen kids?"

"Ten. Five boys and five girls."

"God-Almighty! Like having your own baseball team!"

"But don't you come from a big family too?"

"Yeah. My Granma Jones in Virginia had fifteen and my momma had nine, but three died. But they could afford them. I mean, they didn't go out at all hours to fish . . ."

"Clam."

"Clam, Damn! My Granny had her own business, I mean a still. Sold moonshine all round the state."

25

"Oh yeah? You never mentioned that."

"Ain't nothing to brag about. Worked like dogs, all of them. Up all night, lugging all that stuff. God, I sure didn't envy them."

"Sounds tough."

"Yeah, everybody pulled together in the old days. Even the little kids were used as lookouts."

"Lookouts?"

"Yeah, for government agents. Why my daddy used to tell stories that would drive you wild! I mean, they worked like dogs, just like dogs."

"Oh!"

"Ummm, this sure is the life. Nothing to do but eat, sleep and . . ."

"Tequila, anyone?"

"I'm drinking beer, Biff."

"Beer! Shit, beer's for daytime. Tequila is for night time. Yessiree, goes down just like . . . Say, David, when you figure they'll have light, I mean 'lectricity in this place?"

"The line's up to the road, but not the regular homes."

"Look, Daddy, a falling star!"

"I can see Ursa Major, Stacey."

"Sure is quiet around here, David. What do people do here at night, I mean with no t.v. or radio, I mean . . ."

"Just go to bed, Biff. Most get up early for work."

"Ha, ha. Go to bed to make more kids, you mean. Aha, ha. Hey, Bitsey, wanna go back to our ole camper and do something?"

"No way, Biff, no way am I gonna be round a man smelling of beer."

"Tequila."

"Buenos dias, David. Aqui le traigo leña."

"Gracias, gracias, Don Timoteo. Mire, le presento mi neighbor, uhh vecino. Biff, this is Mr. Timoteo. Este es Biff."

"Beef."

"No, Biff. Buuuueeef."

"Pos, eso dije: Beef."

"Howdy, you all. Mucho, how you say? Glad to meet you. Nice place you got here. Pretty. Bonita?"

"Si, señor Beef. Que se diviertan."

"Uhhh, how about some tequila, Mr. Tom-atoe?"

"No *tanks yous*. Es muy temprano. David, voy a mandar a mis muchachos con la burra para que los niños se entretengan, eh?"

"Si. He's sending his boys down with the donkey for the kids to ride."

"Fer how much?"

"For nothing. He's being courteous."

"Yeah?" Never heard nobody not charge for pony rides. I mean, I pay ten bucks an hour just so Bitsey can ride an old mare and . . ."

"These people have a different value system, Biff. I mean, they aren't all out for the dollar . . ."

"Ha, I'll bet. But no offense meant, amigo. Bitsey, Bitsey honey, you all get your boots on. They're coming with a burro so's you all can ride . . . for free!"

"Como te llamas?"

"What is she saying, Mommie?"

"She is asking for your name."

"Oh! Stacey. And you?"

"Blanca Rosa."

"Mommie, what shall I call her?"

"Call her by her name: Blanca Rosa. It means White Rose."

"Oh, that's so pretty. And what does my name mean?"

"Stacey? Well nothing, really. It's just . . ."

"Nothing? Why, Mommie? Why does my name mean nothing?"

"Well, because it's an American name, and Americans don't put much thought into names. I wanted to name you Estrella. It means star, but your dad wanted an American name, so you became Stacey."

"Is Carlos an American name?"

"No. I made sure of that."

"Is your name American too?"

"No, it's really Ave. A-Veh, like in the prayer."

"Then, how come everyone calls you Abby?"

"Well, because it's easier and . . ."

". . . American?"

"It sure is. Tell you what, you call me Ave and I'll call you . . ."

"Star?"

"Yes. Estrella. Ess-tray-ya. Got it?"

"Av-eh, Av-eh. And Ess-tray-ya."

"Estrella. Star. Star-of-the-Sea!"

"Wow!"

"Them kids sure are smart, Abby, especially that White Rose. Why she's as smart as a whip!"

"Yes, the school system's different here. In a way it's more advanced."

"Oh, yeah? They got a school system? Here?"

"Yes. The yellow building over there is the school, *la primaria*, that is: elementary school. Then there's the *secunda-*

ria, similar to junior high; then *la preparatoria* is like high school or college prep. Kids here take G.E. classes at the high school level and when in college they concentrate on their major and . . ."

"Well that's no fun. I mean: what about fun? Football? Cheerleading? I mean, shoot! My last year in high school I had me two classes of drill team, two of dancing and art. I had the best time evehhh!"

"Yeah, but here they take education seriously."

"Oh yeah? How come?"

"Because so few get an education, that's why. When they finish *la primaria*, if they're lucky, they go to school in Santa Maria. That's about ten miles away, past town."

"And if not?"

"Then they stay home and clam."

"Humm. Say, I noticed the kids aren't in school today. Why is that?"

"The scoolteacher didn't show up. It seems he recently got married and, uhhh, I guess he overslept . . . or something."

"So, what do the kids do then?"

"Wait around until he does show."

"Oh!"

"Well, folks, it's our last night here. Sure had me a good time. Good fishing, plenty of beer, and best of all: all that tequila. I'm already on mah last bottle. Gotta pick up some more on the way home. Bitsey, honey, pass the bottle, will ya? Come on, Ab, have some. Take it with lemon, that's it, that's it."

"Really, Biff, anyone would think you discovered tequila."

"Hey, Abby, show us your sketches. She's really good, David. Come on, Abby, show them the one of the clamdiggers."

"I tore that up, Bitsey."

29

"What? That was the best! The shadowing, the light, all them folks. You mean you don't want to show them people like a work of art? Why they'se all as pretty as a picture, ain't that right, Biff?"

"Yup."

"That is known as romanticizing."

"Oh?"

"Come on, Abby, give us all that Third World shit. I tell you, college sure has changed you."

"David, what you and Bitsey and Biff call beauty, art is not. Not really. It's the reality. I mean you think it's graceful, artistic, but all that shit, I mean all those words *is* romanticizing, distorting the reality, making suffering look noble, artistic, uhhhh . . ."

"Tequila, anyone?"

"Sure, why not?"

"Daddy, are we almost to the bad part?"

"We went past it already, while you were asleep. We're now at the border. Remember to let me do the talking, okay?"

"Are they gonna stop us?"

"No. We're Americans. Besides, we don't have any . . ."

"Guns?"

". . . guns or stuff like that. Liquor, firecrackers."

"But I saw you hide some bottles in the dirty clothes, and Biff put lots of tequila inside the camper toilet."

"Well, just be quiet. Yes, sir, American citizens here. Just been . . ."

"Pull over."

"What? We're Americans and . . . Okay, okay! Dammit, Abby, why us? I mean just look around. They're only pulling over us dark-looking folks. Look over there . . . and there.

All Mexicans, uhhh Chicanos. Dammit, now I'll miss the Rams game. Shit!"

"Daddy, the Johnsons just went by. How come they didn't get stopped?"

"Cause they're white, stupid."

"Daddy, Carlos called me stupid. He said . . ."

"Shut up, Stacey. Dammit, Abby, I don't wanna pay a fine. Shit!"

"Sir?"

"Yes, sir!"

"Just open the back door. The missus and kids can get off and wait over there. Hummm, what is this?"

"A sack of dirty clothes."

"Hummm. There appears to be bottles too. Well, well, . . ."

"Shit."

"Got anything else hidden?"

"No, sir. I swear it. These are just gifts for friends, my boss . . ."

"Well, well, what have we here? M-100's? Firecrackers? A nice little arsenal! These wouldn't happen to be your son's?"

"Carlos, where did you get these?"

"Where you got the tequila."

"Just follow me to the office, folks. We'll fill out the forms, then you pay the fine and you can be on your merry way."

"Daddy, are you going to jail?"

"Carlos, how could you? Haven't I told you it's against the law?"

"What law?"

"Dammit. Fifty dollars! And they kept my tequila! Dammit, Abby."

"Daddy, look. It's the Johnson's. They waited for us. Aren't you gonna stop?"

"No."

"Biff and Bitsey get to keep all their tequila."

"They can have it."

Epilogue: School assignment: September, 1979

What I Did This Summer

by Stacey Garcia

This summer me, my brother Carlos and my mommie and daddy went to Mexico. We had fun in the camp. The first day we put up the tent and ate hot dogs. The next day we met some Mexicans who were so poor my mother painted their picture and gave them cookies. We ate lots of clambs and I got to riede on a donkey named Elihio. My best friend is a girl named White Rose in American and Blanca Rusa in Mexican. She and I played all the time. She had long black hair that she let me comb. She was crying when we left the clambs so I gave her all my bubble gum.

On the way home to our house we almost got rested because we had some tequila and bombs inside the dirty clothes but we didn't. My father got real mad cause we were Americans and it wasn't fair but my mother thought it was funny.

I collected shells and sand-dollars. I got bit by three ants and five mosquitos. In Mexico my names is Asstraulia which means Star and is not Stacey. We got to stay up late and I saw Ursa Major. My daddy and Mr. Biff drank lots of tequila and we all had a good time.

School assignment: September, 1979

"My Summer Vacation"

by Carlos Garcia

This summer we went camping to San Quintin in Baja California del Norte. We went with our neighbors the Johnsons and stayed at the beach near the family of Mr. Tomateo.

On the way past Tijuana we saw lots of people and cars. And kids.

We went fishing every day. I caught three croakers and five perch. I went clamming at night with my friend Norberto from the ejido (which is a town). Clamming at night is fun sometimes, but the water was too cold. I gave Beto my fishing boots and I let him have all my clams to fill up the sacks. They took them to Ensenada. I got to ride a burro. It was fun at first, but when he threw me off three times, I quit.

I went hiking with my mother. She was looking for something to paint. I saw a flintswift lizard and caught a horny toad, but let him go.

The school was closed for two days, so my friends and I

went swimming. Mrs. Timateo sent us some tortillas and my mother sent her cookies. Then she sent us some chili and my mother sent her some jam.

My sister got bit by some ants and Mr. Johnson got sunburned because he drank lots of tequila. Bitsey rode the burro all day.

The people here are very poor. They dig for clams almost every night, even the ladies, but they are all friendly and share their food. I gave my books to my friend Fidel who made me a map of Baja. Next year when I go back I will clam some more and show the donkey who is boss. On the way home I slept all the way past the border.

La Josie

La Josie

Yesterday I saw la Josie. She was in the Safeway, plucking chiles *güeritos* from a vegetable bin. Although I had not seen her for years, I recognized her immediately. She had changed very little; she was a bit heavier perhaps. But I knew it was her. The small, brown face, piercing eyes, magenta lips were unchanged. Her formerly blue-black hair, now a blend of white roots and black curls, was swept up in a 1940s pompadour. From her small ears gold earrings sparkled as she moved around crates of potatoes, tomatoes and *cilantro*. She wore a red cotton dress. Her bare feet, in matching thongs with purple toenails, were a sight to behold. The once shapely legs bulged with blue-green veins. I watched her for a minute then walked toward her. Just as I came close she looked up, turned and went off in another direction.

I first met la Josie when I left the sanitarium where I had spent a year with tuberculosis and had moved into an apartment next to hers. At twenty-two I was the divorced mother of a four-year old son, my sole responsibility, for whom I cried during the first lonely days of my confinement. Upon leaving the sanitarium I immediatly looked for an apartment near my only sister, Veronica, or Ronnie as I called her. I needed her to drive me to the store, laundromat, and for moral support. It was urgent I find an apartment near a school. My son would begin kindergarten in the fall. After a one-week search (that left me exhausted and depressed), I moved into the one apartment I could afford: one half duplex on a weed-covered lot. I took with me the few pieces of furniture stored in Ronnie's garage, some pots and pans . . . and my child.

La Josie lived in the next apartment with Peter, her husband, and three-year old child, Anita. Josie was of medium height and weight. Her clear olive skin was decorated on one cheekbone with a tiny blue-black cross. She was most un-friendly. She never returned a hello or smile. She would how-ever send Anita to borrow an egg, sugar or milk at least once a day. Josie would remain indoors most of the day; but I knew she was home because of the blare of the radio that shook the thin wall separating us.

The radio went on at five-thirty each morning. *El Noticiero Mexicano* screeched out timely announcements of fiestas, fu-nerals, and food specialties at Don Jesus' Meat Market. Later I could hear the sound of their car starting up followed by shouts of "Here's your lunch, honey." Then all would be si-lent until about then when once again the radio blared forth *corridos* and northern Mexican style music.

I first met Pete, Josie's husband, one Saturday night about a month after having moved in. I had bathed and put my son to bed, then sat to read a while. I was still on medication and tired easily. Later I too went to bed. I was sound asleep when I awoke to a loud knock at the back door. I ignored this; I knew no one in the area, but the knocking continued, hard, insistent. Then I heard someone shout: "Elen, Elen, open the door." I sat up, grabbed my robe and walked on bare feet to the back door.

"Who is it?" I asked, hand tight on the door. "Who is it?"

"It's me. La Josie. Open the door. Come on."

I stood still, my heart pounding, then tiptoed to check on my son who was sound asleep.

"Elen," the voice was thick, slurred. "Elen, abre la puerta, open the door. It's me, Josie."

I stood and waited . . . and debated. It *was* three in the morning; I was alone. I pulled back the chain and slowly opened the door.

"Where's the phone?" demanded Josie, pushing past me into the bare living room. "Gimme the phone. I gotta call the cops."

"The cops?" I clutched my robe tight. "The cops?"

"Yeah. I'm gonna put the cops on Pit. *Ese cabron.* "Here," she ordered me to the phone. "Dial their number, go ahead."

Just then we heard a cry from the door. Anita stood crying and shivering: "Mommy, I'm scared."

"Chut up," screeched Josie. "Shut your mouth." She stood near the phone, a Lucky Strike clutched in fingers that shook as she re-dialed the number. When she failed to reach the operator, she angrily turned, thrust the phone into my hand and said: "Here, Elen, you do it."

Through a cloud of smoke I swiftly dialed the emergency number. I felt nervous and frightened around Josie. I could smell the beer, her perfume . . . her anger. The pompadour now hung across her flushed face. Her eyes, framed beneath pencil-thin eyebrows, glittered dangerously. The black satin blouse was pulled to one side.

"I'm gonna get him this time. Wait till the cops get here," she hissed as I continued to dial. As she moved towards me we heard a car come up the driveway. It was him! El Pit! Josie quickly dropped the phone, dashed to the door, switched on the porch light, pulled the chain across the opened door. We stood close, the smooth satin of her blouse rubbed against my thin chenille robe. The car door opened; out came a tall, well-built man who even in the dark appeared handsome. We stood and watched as he walked toward us. To *my* door!

The porch light shone on a strong face topped by a large cowboy hat. He wore dark pants and pointy cowboy boots. He put one foot on the stoop, then stood there quietly. Inside Josie, suddenly alert, puffed on a cigarette. I pressed tight against the door, shivering in my thin robe, my hands clammy, throat tight. We peeked and waited until he turned and walked toward his own door.

El Pit had gone but a short distance when suddenly Josie pushed me aside, swung the door wide open and shouted: "So you're finally here, cabron! Just in time. They're coming for you now." She thrust her hand out, fingers bunched together into a fist. Pete kept on walking. Josie's voice grew louder, the cigarette about to burn her fingers. She screamed once more: "Don't tell me you're scared of *me*?" The tall figure continued to move away. Josie, now on a roll, visibly agitated, screeched, "Go ahead, run chicken." She flung open the door, stalked out to the porch and screamed: "You hear, Pit . . . the cops are coming for you now. You'll see cabron. You don't have papers . . . they're gonna send you back . . ."

She never finished. Pete stopped, turned around and came straight to the door, but Josie, equally fast, slammed it shut. She pulled the chain across once more, then, secure behind the door, continued to berate him. When he did not answer, she quieted down, lit another cigarette and blew smoke in my face as we waited to see what would happen next. Soon after, we heard their car start up and drive away, el Pete at the wheel. Josie then grabbed Anita, stubbed out her cigarette in a coffee cup and left. I quickly locked the door behind her, changed my clothes and called my sister Ronnie who sent her sleepy husband to pick up my son and me.

The next morning I returned to pick up our church clothes. I walked cautiously past Josie's apartment. I could smell *chorizo* cooking. On the porch stoop was the man I had glimpsed the night before, sitting in an old metal chair, Anita on his lap. From the doorway a smiling Josie looked down at them. She wore the same satin blouse. The pompadour was once again high, elegant. I smiled, murmured "hi," but she averted my glance. Her dark eyes were riveted on her man, el Pit, who from all appearances was home to stay.

In the following months more fights took place, with some variations. Josie and Pete would drink, argue. Then he would chase her across the way to my half of the house. Usually she called out to me while running up the driveway, dash in and lock the door in Pete's face. When we heard their car drive away she would unlock the door . . . and go home.

At times the fights began on Friday night. The thin walls vibrated with a profusion of sounds: music, laughter, followed by shouts of *cabron*, the scraping of chairs and slamming of doors. By Saturday the real partying began. The small apartment bulged with *compadres* and *comadres*, beer, *menudo*, pigs feet. The noise continued till dawn. More than once I awoke tired and sleepy. Only my son slept soundly, unmindful of the outside world. The next day Josie's apartment was deathly quiet. Dark window shades covered the bedroom window. On the front stoop Anita played quietly with her dolls.

One cold Saturday night la Josie came running to my door, Pete hot on her heels. I automatically opened the door and just as swiftly drew the chain across, then put on my robe. Josie said not a word, but went straight to the phone. She then remained sitting at the kitchen table, a cigarette in her hand, until Pete drove off. She stretched, got up and went home. It never occured to her (or me) to cancel the emergency call.

Within minutes a police car screeched up the driveway, it's red lights glowing in the dark. I heard voices, footsteps, then a knock at my door. While making the telephone call, Josie had given *my* name, *my* address. I stood in my thin robe to explain to the uniformed men the circumstances that had led to the call, as nearby neighbors stuck their heads out to see the trouble. The policemen left to talk once more to Josie, then returned to say she denied having called them! Worse, she insisted I had been drinking and fighting with my boyfriend. The police, assured perhaps by my disheveled appearance and frantic protestations, finally left. I went back to bed furious at Josie, furious at myself. On the following weekends I began to stay overnight at my sister Ronnie's house. I did not fear Pete, nor the police, but Josie. During the day, when we met near the garbage cans, she never spoke other than to snarl: "Hi!" And then one warm sunny day I moved away.

I was re-instated at my old job, rented a nice two-bedroom apartment and enrolled my son in kindergarten. I also bought a used car and couch and tried to get on with my life. Now and then, on my way to visit Ronnie, I drove by the duplex . . . and looked the other way. It hurt to remember that frightening time in my life when everything was uncertain, when I hated the bare, shabby apartment, the drunken fights, la Josie, el Pete.

A year later I married a man I had met at a Little League game. He was a baseball coach. I felt he liked kids and would surely love my son. We moved to Happy Acres where I later gave birth to another son and became immersed in PTA and Boy Scouts. I often visited Ronnie. It pleased her that I was no longer alone, a divorcee. I was now married. Secure. No longer forced to leave my home in the middle of the night due to a neighbor's drunken brawl. We rejoiced at my good fortune.

Then Ronnie became ill, seriously ill . . . and my life began to fall apart. My husband discovered he didn't really like children. He hated baseball too. The close family I had envisioned did not materialize. He began to work overtime, at first only Saturdays, then Sundays too. I felt I could not complain, after all, he *was* supporting a child that was not his! Then the phone began to ring at odd hours, the muffled conversations cut short when I appeared. He let his hair grow long, bought an herbal shampoo and informed us it was for his use only.

He next bought a hair dryer and spent hours blow-drying his rich, shoulder-length hair while the boys and I waited to use the bathroom. He also bought tight jeans which I washed in hot, hot water to make them tighter, and wore cotton shirts embroidered with butterflies, and a necklace of colored beads. And then one day he told me he wanted a separation. A "trial" separation. "I'm almost forty," he hissed. "I need to find myself," while I, at thirty-five, thought I knew where I was.

We went to see a marriage counselor but soon quit. He said there was nothing wrong with *him*! We went to see a divorce lawyer. He assured me that having the same lawyer would save us money, and, since I had none of my own, I agreed. After a time we got a divorce. A friendly divorce. We sold the house. I kept the battered station wagon, some pots and pans and the kids. He got his new Porsche, a set of wine glasses and the hair dryer. I began to look for a job. Just when I was getting desperate, I was rehired at my old job. I immediately lost ten pounds, bought a three-piece suit, then farmed out the kids to various sitters. I spent weekends with Ronnie, now near death. She did not know my situation, but smiled when during a visit I left early. Surely I was going home to cook dinner.

The days and months dragged like years. I hated the small apartment. It was too far from schools! I hated my old car, the shabby furniture. Mostly, I think, I hated myself. The children somehow survived the turmoil, the confusion . . . my guilt. We hardly ever saw my "ex." I heard he had an apartment with a seventeen-year-old girl he met at a ball-game! A tall, skinny blonde who one day took off with the Porsche. Later he moved in with an older woman who bred horses. I thought I saw him once atop a Palomino, riding off into the sunset. He had found himself at last when the horse had thrown him and he ended up in the hospital. I, as next of kin, was summoned. He recovered in record time . . . then moved away.

Yesterday I saw la Josie. I caught up with her near the market exit. I was about to call to her when I moved aside to let a tall, handsome, grey-haired man wearing cowboy boots pass. It was him! El Pit! He went past, a six-pack tucked under his arm, to where Josie waited. "Here you go, honey," he said, handing her the beer. She smiled at him, her dark eyes softened. Then, arm in arm they walked to their car, got in and drove off. I stood against the wall and watched as they went past me, close together in the front seat, laughing aloud, happy.

Yesterday I saw la Josie . . . and I saw myself.

Rosa la Cantinera

Rosa la Cantinera

What I remember the most about Rosa Bustamante, known as *la cantinera*, was her generosity. She gave away food, beer, and to the children of the barrio, hard candy that she carried in her dress pocket.

I saw Rosa at least once a day, usually in the evening on my way to the corner store when she would stand outside in front of the restaurant. The sign above the door read: ROSITA'S CAFE, and it flickered off and on in the early twilight, outlining her ample figure. The lights went on promptly at five o'clock to remind the working men of the barrio that Rosita awaited them inside the sparkling clean diner with huge pots of *pozole*, tripe stew with hominy.

Rosita, or Doña Rosa as she insisted we children call her, was of medium height and weight. Her skin was the color of ripe apricots. A row of freckles swept across the nose and overlapped onto her generous cheeks. She wore her curly brown hair parted in the middle and secured with ivory combs. Her light brown eyes were friendly. She smiled often, especially at us kids, and at the skinny dogs for whom she saved *patas de cochi*, the pigs feet used in the *pozole*.

What most fascinated me about Rosa was her small nose. It was smaller than my doll's nose and smaller than my thumb. It sat on her face like a tiny blob with two little holes for nostrils. The neighborhood kids argued that she resembled a Pekinese dog. I wondered how she could breathe. The men called her Rosa or Rosita. The women referred to her as *la cantinera*.

Rosa lived alone in two rooms above the restaurant. We knew she was from Mexico but she had no immediate family we knew of in the area. The neighbors called her *una mujer sola*, a woman alone . . . so that we kids thought something was missing in her life. But when I saw Rosa in front of her restaurant she appeared to have everything. Health, freckles and her own business.

Rosa's place was once a tortilla bakery that moved to Van Nuys Boulevard (where small stores opened and closed without notice). When the ugly, grey building was left empty, she quickly bought the place, then fixed it up. From the start the menu was kept simple, featuring only *pozole* and *cocido* accompanied by thick tortillas made with wheat flour, each of which appeared to weigh a ton. All the food was cooked by Rosa. The simple menu, tasty food and reasonable prices appealed to the big, boisterous men dressed in blue denim pants and shirts, all of whom looked like truck drivers. By early evening the restaurant was full of people. That is, men. No women were ever seen at Rosita's.

At first Rosa served the men on long wooden tables pushed against the wall where they sat hunched over, the steam from the *pozole* warming their worn, tired faces while the hot tortillas filled their bellies. Rosa, her face a rosy red, bustled around waiting on the men, bowls of *cocido* and stacks of tortillas balanced on her ample arms.

Most weekends the restaurant bulged with workers in clean, white shirts, dark gabardine pants and hair shining with layers of brilliantine. Business quickly grew; Rosa added more tables and benches, and, later, another room. Cement was poured and a roof added to the small porch, now called a patio. Palm fronds on top of the roof gave it an exotic, tropical effect. On warm nights the men's laughter blended with Rosa's merry peal. And then suddenly, the restaurant closed.

We first knew the restaurant was closed when a sign that read CLOSET was hung on the door. The sign, painted by Don Guzman (who lacked English) was read with curiosity by both adults and children. The restaurant remained closed, as the rumor flew that a health inspector from city hall had been alerted to the possibility of unsanitary conditions by a certain

Joe who found a cockroach in his soup, a charge heatedly denied by Rosa. Others said the inspector was bribed by a jealous wife whose husband was consumed by Rosa's *cocido*.

Within a week the front windows were broken. Tall weeds sprouted near the door while skinny dogs hung around waiting for a stray bone. And then one sunny day Rosa returned.

The neighborhood kids were first to spot Doña Rosa. She stood at the door as though she had never left. The word was passed around. Doña Rosa was back! We quickly lined up for candy; the dogs whined for *patas*. The cafe underwent a renovation. The building was stuccoed and painted a bright green. The front windows were widened so that from the sidewalk we could see the inside clearly. The patio was enclosed, the palms replaced by a plastic roof. The new neon sign (said to have cost all of fifty dollars) now said: ROSA'S RESTAU-RANT & BAR. Even the tall weeds where winos peed were replaced by healthy green shrubs. Inside, Rosa could be seen supervising the work, her wide smiling face full of freckles and good will.

The renovation continued. Rosa issued orders in a loud, clear voice to a carpenter who refused to take orders from a *vieja*, a woman, so he quit and was replaced by another who partitioned the front room and installed a double sink near the back door. The rear was designated as the dining area where sturdy chrome tables and chairs with plastic seats replaced the wood furniture. On top of each table stood a cheap glass vase with rubbery flowers from the five-and-dime. New menus were printed with a cover that depicted a man leaning against a tall cactus. However, what most fascinated us kids was the bar.

The front of the restaurant, now the cantina, appeared dark and mysterious. A wide leather bar filled one wall with red plastic barstools lined up in front. A variety of glasses and bottles of liquor—Jim Beam, Hill & Hill—and a big jar with pigs feet sat on a wide shelf. Above this hung a picture of a half-clad Mexican Indian princess and a young warrior who appeared to tower over her. In the barrio this became a very popular picture, and often graced the yearly calendars donated by local shopkeepers. The picture was said to depict a Mexican legend which made the near naked man and woman almost acceptable. Some whispered that the Indian warrior resembled el Joe who had snitched to the health inspector. On warm nights, when business was slow and Rosa joined the men at the bar for a drink, it was said she gazed at the picture with dark, limpid eyes.

Rosa's Restaurant & Bar officially opened one starry night in September during the Mexican Independence Day celebrations. For the grand opening Rosa hired a cook and one waitress. She presided over the bar. That night the building bulged with men who visited the bar to ogle at the naked Indians, *los encuerados* (as the picture was now called), and to have a drink. They then feasted on what the new menu called *antojitos mexicanos*, Mexican appetizers: tacos, tamales and chile verde prepared by the cook, served by the waitress and supervised by Rosa. That year the excitement of the 16th of September fiestas was intensified by the many fights that broke out at Rosita's.

During the Christmas and New Year's holidays, the restaurant was aglow with the lights from the plastic Christmas tree and the nativity scene atop the bar from where Baby Jesus looked up at *los encuerados*. On New Year's Eve the cafe was jammed with men in shiny gabardine pants and starched white shirts. That night two fights broke out, one inside the bar, said to be over Rosa's affections, and another, a really good one which began on the sidewalk. The men fought with both fists and beer bottles. One flew through the air missing Rosa and *los encuerados*, to make a direct hit on the cook. Because it was New Year's no one thought of calling the cops. The fight continued until everyone was punched out. Afterwards everyone went inside for a bowl of menudo (said to sober one up) and to assess the damage, none of which was insured. The numerous fights and altercations with *la chota*, the cops, earned the restaurant a bad name. The whole town was in an uproar as weekend after weekend new fights erupted in what was now freely called the den of sin.

The women of the Altar Society demanded that our pastor, Padre Juanito, protest the brawls and public shame fostered by alcohol. Rosa, aware of the impending visit, met *el padrecito* at the door dressed in a severe black dress that came to her knees, and a gold cross on her ample chest. She invited him to see the bar and the nativity. She asked him to bless the entire building with holy water. He then declined a bowl of cocido, but accepted a small donation for new altar cloths. It was said that more than once his myopic eyes strayed at the picture of *los encuerados*. He later assured the Daughters of Mary that Doña Rosa was a most generous Catholic who even kept a nativity creche in the bar. The women, however, refused the donation and continued to regard Rosa as a bad woman, *una cantinera*, who should be run out of town.

In the following months fights broke out at Rosa's eatery almost on schedule. Chicken wire was nailed to what remained of the windows. Broken chairs were mended with black electrical tape and heavy twine. The nativity was replaced by plastic fruit that fooled more than one drunk. Rosa no longer stood by the door. She was now stationed behind the cash register next to the bar, a loaded 22 rifle tucked under the counter. The young barrio kids no longer dallied near the door waiting for a treat. We now dashed by, fearful of a flying bottle, a crashing chair.

That Spring Rosa expanded the business. She brought in a partner, a certain Manuel. She introduced the burly, stocky man as her partner and future husband! The fights soon ceased; business picked up. No one cared to tangle with a man said to have been a boxer in Mexico. The whole town settled down; the restaurant regained a measure of respectability.

One Saturday night, just before closing time, a woman claiming to be Manuel's wife came to the restaurant accompanied by six children. She stood, illuminated by the lights, calling out: "*Ay, viejo*! Your children are hungry!"

A furious Rosa demanded Manuel to tell the woman to leave. Just then the woman sent the eldest child, a skinny boy, to plead her cause. By now a crowd had gathered; business picked up. Not sure of what to do, Rosa invited the woman and children inside. She fed them *cocido*, packed tortillas and meat in a dishtowel, then shooed them out the back door. Later that night her screams could be heard above the music of the Trio Los Panchos that blared from the jukebox. Soon after, Manuel was seen leaving, a small suitcase tucked under his arm. In the restaurant, a somber Rosa continued with the business.

The town's people now frowned at Rosa more than ever. They discussed the fights and Manuel's wife, and began to refer to Rosa's Restaurant & Bar as a common beer joint. Worse, Rosa was labeled a loose woman, a homewrecker who had taken a man from his family. The eatery, no longer frequented by workingmen, was now patronized by *pachucos* and *braceros* or wetbacks, as we called them. The jukebox was disconnected, the broken windows boarded up. Rosa appeared wan, like the dying shrubs. She no longer smiled at us kids nor saved bones for the dogs, but appeared tired, cross. And then one day above the restaurant sign a new sign appeared which said: *Closed for Repairs*. Rosa, tired of the fights and decline in business, and, smarting from the rejection of the donation for cloths, moved to salvage what remained of her cafe . . . and reputation.

The next time we looked, the former cantina sported a new sign: ROSA'S MEXICAN FOOD. In a few short weeks Rosa changed everything. The partition was removed and replaced with long wooden tables and chairs. Beer was served only with dinner. Rosa fired the waitress and changed the menu.

She now cooked and served her speciality to a new crowd, mostly old men who shuffled in each evening. The braceros stayed away; they loved the food but feared *la migra*, the immigration authorities. During Christmas and New Year's many had been arrested and later deported. The *pachucos* stayed away from Rosa's. Now and then an old client drifted in for a fast bowl of *cocido*. He kept one eye on his food, the other on the door leading to the street.

Inside the restaurant an older Rosa kept pace with the customers, and outside the door old dogs slept soundly, satiated with leftover pigs feet. Rosa no longer wore brightly colored dresses nor smiled as much. She did, however, make small donations to the church for candles and flowers, but she was never accepted by church-going women that blessed themselves and turned up their nose when they walked past the former cantina. It was rumored that Manuel had returned to his wife and children. The health inspector retired, replaced by a younger, more honest man. And then a new sign in big, bold letters appeared which said: SOLD. As in the past, the children who daily trekked to the corner store to return coke bottles were the first to spot the sign. We ran around to the back entrance. It too was locked, the windows barred. In the rooms above the old building, dusty white curtains stuck to the cracked windows.

Later we heard that Rosa had returned to Mexico to live out her life, stung by the criticism and rejection of the townspeople. The restaurant, its paint chipped and dry, remained empty. The boarded-up windows had seen the last of flying beer bottles. The Daughters of Mary, paragons of virtue, finally accepted Rosa's donation. The kids and dogs of the barrio she befriended were the only ones to miss Rosa la cantinera, one of the lone women that lived in our town.

El Marxista

El Marxista

Concha pulled into the wide driveway, her eyes glazed from staring into the retreating Tucson sun. She turned off the ignition, jerked out the key, jumped out of the car, then walked around to the rear, opened the car trunk, propped the piece of wood kept in the trunk between the broken hinge and began to unload. Damn, Concha hissed, I'll have to remind Carlos to please (please honey!), have the car trunk repaired. But just now she felt exhausted, beat. I've spent the whole damned day with that snotty asshole, she grumbled. The whole damn day spent shopping with Don Francisco Corriente, the so-called distinguished scholar from Latin America. She pulled packages from the car trunk, thinking of how much her political perceptions had changed since Don Francisco's arrival. It had begun innocently enough with the telephone call from her chairman.

When the call from Dr. Bellcrom came, Concha was delighted to hear him invite her to participate in the forthcoming conference on U.S.-Latin American relations. Later, when told she would moderate a panel, not present a research paper, her enthusiasm began to wane. Nor did it help to know that all of the selected speakers were men. Sexist pigs, Concha grumbled, as she typed invitations for the conference long past her work hours. Male chauvinist pigs!

On the day preceding the official opening of the conference Dr. Bellcrom called Concha aside and in a smooth oratory voice said, "My dear Mrs. Gomez-Taniz, I need your assistance. My dear wife is down with the flu and, as you know, Don Francisco Corriente, our featured speaker, was to have been our houseguest. I was wondering if I might impose on you to . . ."

"Yes." The word was out before Concha realized she had uttered it.

"It will only be for two days, er . . . nights. I'm sure he'll be no trouble at all. These poor chaps are pretty easy to please, and you do speak their language, so . . ." Dr. Bellcrom looked at his watch, pressed Concha's hand, slipped on a Harris tweed jacket and, as he approached the door, called out, "His plane arrives tonight, Flight 219, Aeronaves. Check with my secretary. Ciao." His retreating footsteps echoed down the hall.

Concha grabbed her purse, ran to the corner office she shared with three other part-timers and, her eyes on the clock, dialed her husband's office. Already she felt nervous and apprehensive about her guest. Ring, dammit, she hissed to the phone. Ring.

"Carlos, honey, it's me Connie . . ." From experience Concha knew she must first call Carlos honey at least three times before she could ask a favor. "Something's come up, honey. Can you pick up the kids?" There was no answer. She began once more, "Carlos, honey, I've got to run to the market and then to the airport. You've got to pick up the kids by five."

"So who's coming to town?" Carlos asked irritably.

"Some speaker for the conference tomorrow. He's a well known Marxist, from Latin America, I forget his name. He's gonna stay with us for two nights and . . ."

"A communist is staying in my home?"

Concha could envision Carlos in his three-piece suit at his oak desk puzzling over how to act around other than staunch middle-class Americans.

"Well," his voice took on the usual authoritative tone. "I guess we can handle a houseguest, but do I have to feed the kids and all that?"

"Give them soup. I'll be home by nine at the latest."

Concha could barely contain her anger. Shit! In a courtroom Carlos was said to be "hell on wheels." His oratory swayed jurors, but around their kids and especially in the kitchen he acted like an asshole.

"Does this mean I'll have to bathe them too?" His voice boomed across the wires.

"I have to dash, honey. See you at home." Concha slammed down the receiver, grabbed her worn briefcase, coat and purse, and ran out to the faculty parking lot and to her compact car which was wedged between two BMW's. On the way to the market she made a mental note of what foods to buy. My houseguest is an important man. I should have a few goodies on hand, stuff I don't usually buy. Everyone knows that marxists eat common fodder, peasant food, Concha reasoned. I'll fix some really nice dinners to make up for what he eats at home. Even though he's a Communist, uhh marxist, he's gotta eat too. Once inside the market, she whizzed down the aisles, loading the cart with an assortment of goodies: frozen scallops, spumoni, capuccino, artichokes and fresh strawberries. At the checkstand her neighbor Bennie greeted her, then began to bag the food.

"Man, who's coming over? . . ." he asked holding up a can of clams, ". . . President Reagan?"

"No, actually it's Don Francisco Corriente, a marxist, uhhh, socialist from Latin America."

"Oh yeah?" Bennie, an economics major at the university, looked at Concha suspiciously, then walked her to the car.

"Are you sure you won't be harboring a fugitive from justice?" he asked laughingly.

"Does Carlos know this? Is he legal?"

"Cut the crap, Bennie, I'm not in the mood for your editorials." Concha started up the car, then feeling contrite, leaned out the window and yelled, "I suppose you'd like to interview him for your research paper?"

"Yeah!" Bennie's eyes sparkled, "I sure would. And for *La Penca*, too." Bennie, as editor of the Chicano Studies newsletter, often came to Concha for sources. "All them dudes are the same though; all they want is to overthrow the government and . . ."

"Bye, Bennie." Concha headed east toward the freeway. It was rush hour; the freeway was jammed with cars. Dammit, I'll be late, she fumed, digging in her purse for gum. It seemed everyone was heading for the airport too! She glanced at her trusty Timex watch. She had exactly twenty minutes to make it to the airport, park the car and find the correct terminal. Shit, if I'm late, I'll make a poor impression on Doctor Corriente, Concha grumbled irritably, honking at a slow-moving car. She pressed down on the accelerator, cut between a cement truck and emerged triumphantly at the airport entrance with five minutes to spare. Inside the terminal, Concha headed for Gate 8. More than once she and Carlos had delivered his better-heeled (and undocumented) clients to this gate, to be sent home via Mexico. More than once they had stood at the gate wondering when the constant flow of illegals—as the newspapers called them—would lessen. Concha took a deep breath, dashed into the ladies room. There she ran a comb through her hair, washed her hands, dabbed on rouge. Out she came and sprinted up the escalator in time to hear that Aeronaves Flight 219 had just landed.

A huge crowd was gathered in front of Gate 8. Concha strained to see beyond the knot of people ahead of her. God, I hate being so short, she grumbled while standing on tiptoes. I'm sure to miss el marxista. She pushed forward to the front and waited for what she was sure would be a most distinguished Latin-looking man. Maybe he'll be wearing fatigues like Fidel Castro, a real man of the the people. Within minutes the crowd thinned. Passengers met by friends and relatives adjourned to the bar; others marched to the escalators. Still Concha could not make out a distinguished looking man. She was about to have Doctor Corriente paged when she saw a sandy-haired man of medium height and weight approaching.

"Profesora Gomez-Taniz?"

"Yes. Si"

"Soy el doctor Corriente."

"Oh, Uhhh, welcome, Bien venido."

"I speak English too."

"Oh!" Concha blushed as she shook his limp hand.

"This is all I brought with me." Doctor Corriente pointed to a garment bag and a small attache case. "Ready?"

Concha led the way to the car, acutely aware of the importance of the man who followed her out the door and to the parking lot. She made polite conversation, but el marxista appeared distant, aloof. He's probably tired, Concha reasoned. The long trip did him in. A good, hot meal and a warm bath should revive him. She drove carefully, easing the car into traffic with care, not wanting anything to happen to the important personage in her car. They arrived at the compact housing tract just as the street lights went on.

"Here we are," offered Concha, trying not to feel superior. This poor man probably lives in a hut, she sighed, a man of the people who shares not only ideology but the hardships of life. She parked the car in the driveway, opened the trunk, propping it up with the wooden block and then yanked out the grocery bags. With her purse and coat dangling to the pavement, she groped her way to the kitchen door. From the den the children's voices could be heard above the din of the television set.

"Honey, I'm home. Carlos?"

"Daddy's asleep, Mommy."

Concha motioned to el marxista to put down his garment bag. She woke Carlos up, who immediately sat up, extended his hand and waved el doctor Corriente into the living room. Carlos excused himself to go into the kitchen.

"Beer? Uh, una cerveza?"

"No, gracias, es que . . ."

"Honey, I bought some Scotch. It's right here," called Concha from the kitchen. "Fix us a highball. Use the glasses in the china closet, the ones we got for Christmas." Carlos walked into the kitchen, stared at the bottle of Chivas Regal, spun it around to see the price tag, then aware that Concha was watching, went into the dining area and selected highball glasses and returned to the kitchen. "Here, rinse them out."

Concha turned around, with a frown on her otherwise pleasant face. She was about to give a smart retort, but remembered they were not alone. This was not the time to be a women's libber. She took the glasses to the sink, rinsed and dried them and then handed them to Carlos, who shook out ice cubes, fixed drinks, and walked back into the living room. The marxista was sitting in Carlos' favorite chair, his soft leather shoes resting on the embroidery of the footstool sewn by Concha. Carlos, a frown on his face, looked at el marxista, raised his glass and said, "Salud."

"Cheers."

In the kitchen Concha scurried around trying to locate her recipe for veal scallopini. She had asked the butcher to slice the baby veal especially thin, and was now ready to saute the fresh mushrooms and scallions in real butter. She called out to Carlos: "Honey, have the kids eaten?"

"Nah, they weren't hungry. I took them to MacDonalds for chocolate sundaes."

"Yes, but did they eat food?"

"That's food."

Visibly irritated, but conscious of their guest, Concha decided to postpone the discussion on the kids. Just now she would have to concentrate on the veal. She worked swiftly, eyeing the clock until Sergio, her six year old, wandered into the kitchen, his hand on his stomach.

"Mommy, I feel sick. I think I'm going to throw up."

"Quick, to the bathroom. Carlos," Concha called, her voice shrill. "Sergie is sick, and wants you." She was furious at Carlos for not giving the kids solid food. "Carlos, can you please take Sergie?" Concha, determined not to call Carlos "honey," held her breath and called out.

"Sergie's going to . . ."

Concha did not finish. As she yanked Sergie toward the bathroom, he vomited on the kitchen floor. Concha, aware the mushrooms were burning, quickly turned off the stove and then bent down to wipe Sergio's frightened face. She dashed to the sink, poured a glass of water and gave it to Sergie, who immediately spat it out. Meanwhile in the living room, Carlos, visibly relaxed, poured another drink for el marxista, who was still sprawled on the leather chair. Next he poured one for himself.

"That was a nice dinner, honey. We should eat like this more often," said Carlos, as he moved back from the table. He was in an expansive mood, full of Scotch and tender baby veal. He forgave el marxista for sitting in his favorite chair. Now if he could just get out of bathing the kids, everything would be perfect. He smiled at his houseguest, who smiled back.

In the kitchen Concha struggled with the dishwasher, now loaded to the gills with a week's dishes. She felt beat, tired and angry. Dinner had taken her leftover energy, as had cleaning up after Sergie. What really pissed her off was that el doctor Corriente barely touched the veal. "I'm not too hungry," he explained, as Carlos heaped his own plate for the third time. Concha, furious at her guest's lack of courtesy, forced a smile while she reached for the Chivas Regal to refill her glass. I'm getting drunk and I'll look like shit tomorrow, but so what? She walked into the den, gently picked up the sleeping Sergio, carried him to his bed, and returned for Jina, her sleeping daughter. Once Jina was tucked into her white canopied bed, Concha walked back into the kitchen and began to clean up. From the living room Concha could hear el marxista and Carlos deep in conversation.

By eleven thirty the kitchen was once more immaculate. Concha went into the spare bedroom, pulled out the sofa bed, took fresh linens from the closet and made the bed. In the master bedroom she yanked the pillows off the bed and put them on the newly made sofa bed. When everything appeared in order, she turned on the nightlamp, pulled down the window shade and returned to the living room. "Your room is ready, Doctor Corriente," she announced. Concha glanced at her watch and was appalled to see it was close to midnight. I want to go to bed, but can't until my guest does. Shit, what if he's a night owl? She stood, yawned and smiled at Carlos, who smiled back. Just then el marxista stood up, shook Carlos's hand and, with a slight bow to Concha, left the room and headed for the guest bedroom. Concha quickly turned the lamps out, secured the front door and started towards the master bedroom, when el marxista returned to ask, "Are there any towels?" Concha, her face a bright pink, quickly dashed to the linen closet, pulled down the new velour towels (a Christmas gift from her sister), handed them to her guest who ran his hand over them appreciatively and said, "These are exactly like the ones we have at home," and turned to enter the bathroom. Carlos shrugged his shoulders, sauntered toward Concha and began to run his hands over her hips.

"Not tonight, Carlos."

"Why not? I'm not tired. I feel great and . . ."

Inside the bedroom Concha quickly undressed, put on a flannel nightgown (a signal to Carlos she was not in the mood to make love), then rummaged in the closet, looking at her outdated wardrobe. Shit, I have nothing to wear. I completely forgot to stop at the cleaners. Dammit, anyway. Concha creamed her face, brushed her teeth and crawled into bed. Well, she sighed, nothing is perfect, not even a houseguest who barely nibbles at my veal scallopini. She snuggled down under the blankets and was about to doze off when she remembered she would have to drive el marxista to campus by ten. So she got up and went back to the kitchen to prepare things for tomorrow. She stacked the dishes still hot from the dryer, re-mopped the sticky floor and began to plan the next day's meal.

The next morning, much to Concha's dismay, the velour towels lay on the bathroom floor. Concha picked them up, shook them out, hung them up, then scoured the washbowl with Babbo, opened the window, fluffed the shower curtains, straightened the bath mat and sprayed the toilet seat with Lysol. She then went into the kitchen where she filled the percolator, arranged bacon on a micro dish, beat eggs, sliced peppers and mushrooms, unwrapped ready-made croissants and finally sat down to wait for her guest who walked in at eight thirty. "May I please have some clean towels?" Concha, trying not to gag on her coffee, walked to the linen closet, pulled out the blue 100% cotton towels bought recently on sale, removed the price tag and handed them to el marxista. Shit, she grumbled, why can't he use the same towels twice? On further reflection, she decided the poor man was entitled to some luxuries. He probably doesn't have indoor plumbing at home, let alone hot running water. I'll try not to let this bother me. After all, today is my day off and I have to enjoy some of it.

Concha dreaded Saturdays. Carlos always found excuses for not helping with the housework or the kids. Last night in bed Concha reminded him of his promise to take care of the kids on Saturday.

"I don't remember promising," Carlos mumbled from beneath the sofa pillows. "I want to play golf."

"This conference is important to me, Carlos. You better not let me down." Concha raised her voice and elbowed him. Sometimes when Carlos acted like an ass, she would give him a quick jab in the ribs.

"Don't hit me anymore, Mommie, I'll do it, I'll do it, but . . ."

"But what?"

"I need a little . . ." Carlos slipped his hand under Concha's nightgown, snuggled close to whisper, ". . . just a little bit to put me to sleep."

"I'm tired."

"Just a quickie."

"Well, hurry up, I've got to get up early."

"Ummmmm."

Early the next morning, just as the alarm went off, Concha heard movement from the guest room. She quickly hopped out of bed thinking that Doctor Corriente sure is an early bird. She then remembered that, as a Marxist, he probably lived very simply: went to bed with the chickens and rose with the dawn. But, she was still irritated. The conference doesn't begin until 9:30 and he's already up, which means I'd better hurry and fix breakfast. She stepped in and out of the shower in record time, put on her underwear, including the torn pantyhose worn the night before, threw on her chenille robe and went to prepare breakfast, one eye on the clock over the stove.

The conference had gone well. That is, once they had arrived, everything had gone smoothly for el marxista, who immediately was surrounded by academics, students and, surprisingly enough, members of the local newspaper. Even Bennie was there; he acted as if he were on intimate terms with el doctor Corriente. But Concha was exhausted, her wool jacket felt uncomfortable, her blouse wilted, her limp hair in disarray. She realized that, as official hostess for this prominent man, she might be expected to ask members of the Poly Sci Department for drinks that evening, but was equally determined to avoid having to "put out," as she called the extracurricular activities women academics were often asked to do. No way, Jose, thought Concha with uncharacteristic hostility. Old man Corriente's already boring me to death. I'll make an effort to leave the conference early and forego invitations for drinks with members of the panel. I'm just too damn tired, she reasoned, thinking back to that morning's events.

That morning, soon after nine, Concha collected her briefcase, scanned her notes, gave Carlos repeated instructions on how to turn on the vacuum, washer and dryer, and reminded him to take the children to catechism and to Little League practice. She warmed up the car, as inside el doctor Corriente sipped a second cup of coffee. She was apprehensive about arriving late, not that anyone would notice. Few participants arrived in time for anything but their own presentation; she too could sneak in and pretend she had been there all along, but she dared not deliver el marxista late. If he were late it would be assumed that Concha could not get her act together. No one would think to blame him. She sat in the car and waited. It was past nine before el doctor Corriente, dressed in a light wool suit and signature necktie came out the kitchen door and briskly walked toward the car. He smiled at Concha, his beady eyes still swollen from sleep. He jumped in the car and stretched out to enjoy the ride to the university.

They drove in silence. Concha wanted to turn the radio on full blast as was her habit, but feared offending her guest. Instead, she pointed out certain landmarks and tried to steer clear of oncoming cars. She was determined not to drive like a mad woman. They were about to enter the freeway when el doctor Corriente turned to her and in a suave voice asked, "Would you be so kind as to take me to a moll?"

"Huh?"

"I want to go to a moll, uhh to the stores."

"Oh! A mall?

"Si, I want to buy some things for my family."

"Sure, there's a Sears nearby."

"How about Magnin's?"

"Well, if there's time."

"Yes, there's time."

Concha swung the car to the right and turned into the parking lot adjoining the newest Tucson shopping mall, an elegant structure called "El Paseo Shopping Mall," known to contain the most expensive stores in the area. She stepped out of the car, followed by el doctor Corriente who immediately passed her, bolted up the escalator and disappeared into a store. Dammit, there's nothing I can afford here, thought Concha pulling at her rumpled skirt. I'll just have to sit and watch the show. She leaned back onto the built-in concrete benches and looked at well-heeled shoppers who rushed in and out of stores, their arms loaded with brightly-wrapped packages. Now and then she looked at her watch and down the walkway, a series of black and white squares with water fountains at each end. I just hope he hurries, she sighed, or we'll never make it. She began to pace back and forth, then gave up and slumped down on the cement and was about to doze off, still exhausted from the strenuous workout of the night before (Carlos' lovemaking), when she saw el doctor Corriente walking toward her, his arms filled with an array of packages. Concha quickly sat up, buttoned her jacket, shifted her purse and prepared to leave.

"My dearest Professor, please watch these things for me. I have to go to another store. I'll be right back." El marxista dropped the packages on Concha's ample lap, turned on his leather heel and once more disappeared down the walkway, his jacket flapping in the breeze.

"Dammit to hell," hissed Concha, digging in her purse for a tissue. This guy is buying out the mall! Just why is he shopping so much? Doesn't he realize only capitalists shop here? Where does he get the money? She counted eight boxes and packages from the best stores in the mall: Joseph Magnins, Joskens, Robesons for Men! Concha sat, fuming, searching in vain for a cigarette in her purse. Perhaps I'm jealous 'cause I only shop in the Sears catalog, she conceded. I shouldn't judge the poor man. Pobrecito. The poor thing is probably buying things for the entire Third World: the hungry, the naked . . . Curious, she peeked inside the heaviest package, then almost dropped it. Inside were two Minolta 35mm cameras, three binocular cases, a Remington shaver, four Sony Walkmans, two bottles of Chanel No. 5 and three bottles of Ralph Lauren's Polo cologne. He sure can't start a revolution with all this, Concha groaned, her eyes popping out of their sockets. Unless he's rich! But her curiosity was aroused. She thought most Marxist officials lived on limited incomes, wore coarse woven clothes, ate dark bread and goat cheese and wore heavy boots. I'm mixing up the Marxists with the Bolsheviks, she sighed, but, dammit, I am curious as hell and would sure like to see what else he's got. She closed the boxes just in time, as round a flowering fuschia bush came el doctor Corrriente at a fast trot. His thin hair was flying, eyes were dilated, his tie askew. In his hands were more packages which he literally threw onto the hard concrete bench. He was sweating profusely, but looking quite content. He sat down next to Concha, smiled into her eyes, pressed her hand, then reached into his jacket pocket for a handkerchief that Concha instinctively knew was silk (and initialed, yet!), then glanced at his watch. "There's still time to go to another 'moll' ", he announced, adjusting his tie. "These stores do not have what I'm looking for. Perhaps we can stop at another place on the way to the university? Perhaps where you shop?"

Concha sat in a trance. Her tired eyes could barely focus on el doctor Corriente who sat next to her looking frantically around, shifting packages, sorting boxes, then once more scanning the different stores. By now she was beyond caring as to whether or not they made it to the conference. She turned to face el doctor Corriente and was about to announce in a controlled voice (the one she used in the classroom) that it was close to eleven, but changed her mind once more. He probably wants all this stuff to sell to the rich and will use the profits to buy rice, or whatever it is people eat in his country. Who am I to deprive him of helping his fellow man? She stood up suddenly, straightened her back and with a bright smile said to el marxista, "Adelante, comrade."

They arrived at the assigned conference room just as the last speaker was winding down. They took their places during the five-minute break allowed for incoming panelists. Concha, suddenly excited, quickly forgot about her wrinkled suit, her swollen feet. Soon all eyes would be on her. By now everyone knew that the distinguished visitor was her houseguest. She felt more important by the minute. When the wall clock struck the hour, she arranged her notes, cleared her throat and began to introduce the topic and, last of all, the male speakers. Polite applause followed each name, but when Concha introduced el doctor Corriente, the assembly rose to its feet; thunderous applause filled the room. From her seat Concha appeared flustered. She clapped softly, without enthusiasm. She stifled a yawn. Her perceptions of Marxism had changed radically. She felt betrayed and, yes, angry at having gone to such lengths to make el marxista comfortable. Hypocrite, she hissed to no one in particular: Hypocrite!

With a polite bow el marxista removed a pair of glasses from his vest. Concha immediately recognized the Christian Dior trademark. He sorted his notes, then thanked the university for the invitation to speak and immediately launched into a litany of abuses committed by the United States against his country. He appeared to choke with emotion as he described the living conditions of *los campesinos*, the lack of water, sanitation and basic foods. He reminded the audience of the great disparity between capitalist and Marxist societies and implied that all of Western Civilization was corrupted by technology. My *compañeros* live in squalid huts, eat one full meal a day, yet do not complain, he screeched, his face a bright pink. He stood on tiptoes gesturing wildly while the audience, in a trance, gaped at him. He concluded by saying he hoped to at least move the people's consciousness about affairs in Latin America, to touch at least one heart, *un corazon*. With a slight bow he sat down to thunderous applause, removed the Christian Dior glasses, then wiped his eyes and brow, while next to him Concha was suppressing a laugh. Once the applause died down the entire panel mixed in with the crowd in the reception hall. Lukewarm wine and the usual cheese and crackers were served. While el marxista spoke with colleagues, Concha looked around for Bennie. Dammit, Bennie was not in the hall! Concha scanned the hallway and stairway. She thought of asking someone to search the men's room, but decided against it. Dammit, Bennie, where are you? Concha nixed the idea of having to find a ride for el doctor Corriente with someone else. It would be impolite. After this emotional evening el marxista would probably like to get home early. Concha, fuming internally, smiled at her colleagues who were busy sipping wine. Just then she saw Bennie approach. She quickly pulled him aside. "Bennie, I need a really big favor."

"Yeah? What's the matter, the CIA on your tail?"

"Knock it off. This is serious."

"So's the CIA, man."

Concha bit her lower lip, swung at Bennie with her purse and was about to use the F word that one never used in public or, Lord forbid, in the classroom. She was pissed. She steered Bennie by the elbow, pushed him out the door and began: "Dammit, Bennie, I've been trying to get you an interview with el . . ."

"Yeah?" Bennie, suddenly alert, popped the remnants of a sandwich into his mouth, then waited for Concha to finish.

"The thing is," Concha whispered inclining her head, "el doctor Corriente has been bombarded with requests for interviews, but I told him that you . . ."

"Far out!"

68

". . . as editor of *La Penca* would be the logical choice."

"You know it!"

"And so, when the reception is over, you're to bring him to my house. But of course you can ask him questions on the way, maybe even use a tape-recorder to save time and . . ."

"Neato, man, I'll take the long way home. Maybe I'll take him to Tudi's Bar for a couple of . . ."

"Better not, Bennie. Tudi's has a bad reputation. Guys get killed every weekend. I can't risk having cops . . ."

"The FBI."

"The FBI, the CIA, los rinches," Concha, aware Bennie was not taking her seriously, leaned close and hissed, "Hey, you wanna be cute or you want the interview?" Now and then Concha had to admit that assertiveness training worked well outside the classroom too. She glared at Bennie who glared right back. Finally Bennie said, "Yeah, well okay. I'll give the dude a ride home. Lucky thing I brought the bug, though the sun roof's stuck and only one door works, but I'll do it, man."

"Shit Bennie, that car's a death trap. Maybe I'd better find another . . ."

"Nelson dijo Wilson."

"What?"

"That's Pachuco jive, man. For being a professor you know nothing about linguistics."

"Linguistics?"

"Socio-linguistics, man. It's the language of the people."

"No shit?"

"Right. For example when I agree with something I say: orale. Or when I disagree or say no I say nel or Nelson." Bennie grinned at Concha, hitched his Levis, then popped an olive into his mouth. "Don't fret your little head, Professor Gomez-Taniz, I'll deliver him home before midnight. Providing my car starts, of course."

Concha felt a sudden pain in her stomach. Holy shit! She

stopped dead in her tracks, looked at Bennie, who made a thumbs-up sign and walked off to find el marxista who was now full of wine and good will and agreed readily both to the ride and the interview with Bennie.

Concha smiled goodbyes to her colleagues, then flew down the stairs and to her car. Once on the freeway she lit a stale menthol cigarette kept hidden from Carlos and the kids in the glove compartment.

She flipped on the radio, kicked off her left shoe and drove home as the white nimbo cumulus that earlier resembled snowcones turned a dark grey. Concha knew it would storm before the night was over.

Now and then Concha glanced at the packages scattered in the back seat, those which had not fit in the car trunk. She no longer felt hostile, but relieved to find them intact, covered with the blanket kept for the children's use. The wine had worked miracles. Concha felt good, proud in fact of how she had deflected questions during the panel discussion and had been alert to trouble-makers who asked pointed questions and had to be immediately cut off. All in all, I did okay, Concha thought. Now all I have to do is put up with el marxista-capitalista (she giggled at this pun) for one more day. Maybe I'll even call in sick on Monday. Take the day off and sleep in. I more than deserve it. She puffed on the menthol cigarette, feeling mellow, and drove home in record time.

It began to drizzle just as the reception ended. Bennie scurried around trying to locate el marxista. If he did not get the VW sunroof covered with the tarp kept for such emergencies, both he and el doctor Corriente would get soaked, which might change the tone of the interview. He scanned the large reception room and zeroed in on el doctor Corriente who ignored him and continued a heated discussion on Marxist theory with important looking men. Bennie, beginning to feel frantic, approached el marxista once more, this time with success. Just then el marxista looked out the window and saw the huge bolts of lightning that accompanied an electrical storm (a thing uncommon in his country) and immediately decided that he would be better off safe at home with such an efficient hostess as la profesora Gomez-Taniz, whom he was sure would not mind fixing a light supper for him. My stomach is more important than a prolonged discussion on Marxist theory, he decided while adjusting his jacket. At least tonight . . . .

Bennie, el doctor Corriente in tow, exited through a side door to be greeted by a huge bolt of lightning, followed by a light drizzle. Instinctively el doctor drew back, but Bennie, determined not to waste time, quickly pushed him on and began to ask pointed questions. He was determined to get specific answers, but found his questions went unanswered each time a lightning bolt appeared. El marxista, his thin face now a ghastly white, kept close to Bennie as they dodged around puddles that were forming in the parking lot.

The purple dented VW shining in the moonlight was known throughout Tucson. Bennie had lovingly painted it a light purple and had had an art student write PURPLE PASSION on each side. This car was his pride and joy. He quickly opened the door, removed the tarp from inside the dented trunk, threw it over the sunroof, tied the ends with twine and jumped in. He then remembered el marxista and got out again to let el doctor Corriente in to the passenger seat. When el marxista was seated, Bennie jumped back in.

Inside the damp, cold car el doctor Corriente huddled next to the door, rainwater seeping over his tweed jacket. He was now sorry he had declined an invitation to sup at one of the better hotels. He had become tired of answering questions and explaining his country's politics. However, he knew the importance of student editors of radical newspapers and was determined to get through the interview.

Once on the highway, Bennie continued to bombard el marxista with questions on Liberation Theology, Opus Dei, literacy programs, human rights, women's rights and foreign policy. Although el doctor Corriente was visibly cold, he tried to give coherent answers. But each time a bolt of lightning struck, el marxista closed his eyes, took a deep breath, leaned back and waited for it to pass. Normally he objected to being interviewed on tape, but today he was too nervous to object. He leaned back onto the cold, wet seat and tried not to mind the loud music that blared from the radio.

The ride home took longer than Bennie expected. The VW had finally started, but was now sputtering and threatening to stop altogether. Dammit, it's gotta be the plugs or the wiring got wet, Bennie groaned softly. I shoulda changed them all. Come on, baby, he hissed, gimme some speed.

I owe it to *La Penca* to get a good interview and to Professor Gomez-Taniz to deliver el marxista back safely, Bennie sighed, ramming the gas pedal. Suddenly the Purple Passion, as though injected with helium, took off. Bennie, confident once more, grinned at el marxista. He lowered the radio and began once more: "So what do you predict will happen when the foreign debt is due?"

"The price of oil will come down."

"And what will that prove?"

"Not much, but soon after we refinance the existing loans the price of oil will go up."

"And what of the poor?"

"The poor we will always have with us."

"Gee, that sounds familiar. May I quote you?" Bennie lowered the radio and was about to repeat the question. Just then a huge bolt of lightning lit up the sky.

"Jesus, Maria y Jose!"

"Do I know them?" asked Bennie, delighted at getting primary sources from such a prominent person. "Could you repeat those names again?"

El marxista, his thin face pale in the moonlight, leaned back into the wet seat. He closed his eyes; he felt sick. When

Bennie repeated the question, he reached into his coat pocket, took out a rumpled paper and handed it across the seat to Bennie. "Use this for your article," he offered. "Feel free to quote me."

Bennie, elated at el marxista's generosity, scanned the article quickly, then picked up speed. Once I'm through with it I'll sell it. Maybe his signature or doodles will bring in some bucks, especially if he becomes their leader, as most of them do. He pulled into Concha's driveway, moved across the cold seat to let el doctor Corriente out, and then with a slight bow, as to royalty, Bennie jumped back inside his battered VW and headed back to campus, to the office that housed *La Penca*.

Early the next morning Concha awoke to hear el marxista in the bathroom. She quickly dressed and still half-asleep, went through the motions of making coffee. She was still tired from yesterday, but was determined to be a good hostess. She set out juice, rolls and then sat down to scan through the newspaper, a luxury she allowed herself on Sundays. Within minutes el marxista appeared.

"Can you please help me pack my, er' these things into boxes? I need some boxes and wondered if . . ." Concha tried not to stare, but did. El marxista was wearing casual clothes: chic, linen slacks and what looked like a Pierre Cardin cardigan. He refused Concha's offer of coffee, saying, "I don't have time. I must put my things in boxes because my plane leaves at two and . . ."

"At two?" Concha almost choked on the coffee.

"Oh, I forgot to mention I cancelled the later flight and will instead leave at two. I was so distracted by the storm, uhhh, conference I forgot to tell you. But I'm sure it's no problem. Oh, and if you could get some tape and ropes and a dark pen . . ." He smiled at Concha, patted Sergie on the head and then went into the living room to watch television with Carlos. "It's obvious he's packed boxes before," Concha mumbled to Sergie. She quickly searched the house for boxes but was unable to find a sturdy one, even in the cluttered garage. She jumped into her car and headed for the supermarkert, the best source for empty boxes. If I hurry I'll be back in time to get him off.

Concha was halfway inside the large garbage bin when she heard a familiar voice say, "God, things are rough all over, Professor Gomez. I thought only bag ladies went through garbage."

"I'm looking for boxes, not food, Bennie." Concha, her face flushed, tried not to laugh. "I need them for el doctor Corriente. He wants . . ."

"Our garbage too?"

"Don't be stupid, Bennie. I need them for packing his things and . . ." Bennie, looking contrite, immediately fished inside the blue bin, pulled out two boxes and handed them to Concha who stuck them in the back seat, smiled her thanks and then drove home, fuming at Bennie, at el marxista and at Carlos who could have at least offered to help. She gave the boxes to el marxista who smiled sweetly and handed them back to her saying, "My dear profesora Gomez-Taniz, I'm going to allow you to pack my things, uh, gifts. Some things we men don't do as well as you women. Somehow we lack the necessary . . ."

Shit, hissed Concha, taking off her jacket. She cleared the kitchen table, rammed packages inside the boxes at random and sealed them with scotch tape at the seams. She was about to secure them with twine when she noticed that the scotch tape was coming apart. Shit, now what will I do? Concha could feel the perspiration dripping from her armpits. Just then Sergie walked in and suggested she use the duck tape kept in the garage. Thanks, genius! Concha hugged Sergie, then asked him to get the tape. Together they sealed the boxes once more and wound each one with twine. Then Concha took a black felt marker and in huge block letters wrote el doctor's name on each box. This done, she rushed to her room and jumped in the shower. By noon she was back in the car, the boxes were in the trunk and back seat and el doctor Corriente sat next to her, a Sony Walkman attached to his ear. At the airport she parked the car, then stood by it until el marxista took the hint, reached inside the trunk while Concha held it open and removed his boxes and garment bag. He carried them inside the terminal; Concha followed, musing at how easy it was to suddenly become a helpless female. When his flight was called el marxista, boxes still in hand, quickly moved forward to stand in line. As he entered the boarding area he paused to adjust the Sony radio, turned back, bowed in Concha's direction, turned and boarded the plan.

Concha drove the long way home. She felt terribly tired, let down, and very, very angry. I've been had, she hissed, stepping on the accelerator. I knocked myself out for el marxista thinking he was a simple peasant. Not only did he reject my veal scallopini, but he left his dirty towels on my clean floors. And all along he wasn't poor at all. He even bragged about how back at home his wife has one maid who does nothing but linens.

Whatta a joke. Maybe, I'm jealous, Concha conceded popping a piece of Juicy Fruit in her mouth. He bought stuff at Joskens while I gotta charge at Sears. What a lot of shit. But next time I'll play it different. Next time I'll tell old Bellcrom to tell his wife to get her ass out of bed and if he asks me to address invitations, I'll bandage my hand and tell him I've got leprosy or something. Then I'll let him know in no uncertain terms that next time I want to present a paper, not moderate a panel, and if he gives me a bad time I'll report him to Affirmative Action. Let him shit in his pants.

She drove, thinking aloud, her hair flying out the window. And another thing, I'm gonna fix Carlos if it's the last thing I do. If he doesn't start doing his share with the kids, I'll cut him off. I'll tell him I have VD or something. And from now on I'm gonna take off on Saturdays and shop. Maybe I'll open a charge at Joskens. If Carlos can buy 100% wool suits why can't I at least buy a nice jacket. Maybe two! She stepped on the gas, her face warmed by the warm sun.

Well, it's over, she concluded turning toward the housing tract and home. Now all I have to do is change the sheets, vacuum the guest room, wash the towels and defrost the scallopini. But for today I'm gonna do nothing but read the Sunday paper. Let Carlos handle the kids for a while. Let him see what it's like to be stuck with them. She lit a stale cigarette, turned the radio on full blast, removed her left shoe and roared down the freeway.

The New Affirmative Action Officer

The New Affirmative Action Officer

He awoke tired. His head ached as did his myopic eyes. The night before he had read the numerous personnel and policy books until late and he was now suffering the effects. As the new Affirmative Action Officer at Jocko Brothers Company he was expected to know, perhaps memorize, the salient points contained in the various manuals.

He struggled to sit up. His short muscular legs were encased in the light cotton pajamas; his hands equally muscular, fidgeted with the alarm clock. A hazy sun hid behind white cumulus, then broke through to light up the small, compact bedroom. A hot, then cold shower failed to revive him. He forced himself to move around the half-empty house, to the wide, pretty kitchen where he fixed a cup of instant coffee and sat down to look out the window. His round face was creased; the laugh lines extended from his brown eyes to the wide mouth that now smiled at the birds awaiting the bread crumbs he had left on the windowsill. He continued to sit . . . and smile. As he sipped the coffee, he thought back to the events that had brought him to this pleasant house, his new job at Jocko Brothers. He thought of wife and daughters back in Kansas. From force of habit he stretched, touched his toes, then headed to the bedroom to dress. On the job for less than two months, he still felt unfamiliar with the company and its policies, but he was determined to succeed. He often reminded himself that he, Albert T. Garcia, had been selected from among the best candidates for this job. He had already made a decision viewed as "fair" by his superiors. He felt bound by the trust and expectations inherent in this most sensitive position, where he would have to mediate between management and employees. He wanted nothing more than to show that he, Albert T. Garcia, first generation Mexican-

American, with an impeccable service record (Korea: 1955) and two college degrees earned at night, could function at this level. He quickly dressed, hung his robe and pajamas on a hook, then placed his slippers under the bed. He felt good wearing the clothes previously selected and packed by his wife. He locked the door and jumped into his dusty blue Volvo for a short drive to the office.

Among the inducements used by the company to get him to move West was the three-bedroom house less than five miles from the job. While in Topeka, during the harsh winter months he often drove in rain and snow for over an hour to reach the office. It was now 8:10 a.m. on a lovely fall day. The road, the tall eucalyptus trees, the bright blue sky were a pleasant sight. Albert felt extremely lucky, . . . and grateful.

Albert T. Garcia turned off the now familiar and less threatening freeway onto the road that led to the plant. He looked up to see that ahead of him in a green Falcon was his secretary: Mrs. Violet Harris, a thin middle-aged woman who ran his office with an iron fist. She had worked at Jocko Brothers for over twenty-five years, first as a file clerk, later in Employee Relations. When new government regulations had made the formation of a new department a company priority, Mrs. Harris had stayed on to work for her former boss, Mr. Pikerton who was now the head of Personnel. She was most helpful; Albert felt lucky to have inherited her expertise. She knew who was important . . . and who was not. Albert thought of her as a good company man, committed to the job. He eased the Volvo into the allocated parking space and noticed that his name, misspelled to read Albert Garcin, had not been corrected. He locked the car door, retrieved his heavy briefcase from the back seat, ran a comb through his thinning black hair and then glanced at his watch. Good! There was time for a fast cup of coffee.

The large cafeteria was crowded. Albert was surprised to see everyone looking so cheerful. It must be the weather that makes everyone seem so alive at this hour, he thought. He moved into line, selected orange juice, coffee and a warm jelly donut from a tray. He sat down at a clean, shiny table to enjoy his food.

As he sipped the hot coffee, Albert smiled at people he thought he knew. He remembered that when he was a child, his mother had scolded him for smiling too much. He straightened up, took a bite from the jelly donut and another swallow of coffee. Albert could never understand why it was considered wrong by some people to smile too much. His former boss had once warned him of this unbusinesslike habit saying, "People don't take you seriously if you smile too much." Only his wife Sonia left him alone. When around Sunny, as he called her, he smiled all the time. Most of the time she smiled back.

Inside the cafeteria, across the room sat a group of young women talking in whispers. Next to Albert three men from the night shift dunked donuts into wide coffee mugs. This seems like a friendly place, Albert thought, slowly chewing the jelly donut, wanting to make it last, beginning to feel the familiar pangs of loneliness. I'm homesick, he admitted, homesick for my wife, my girls and the jelly donuts from Topeka's most popular donut shop. Yes, he thought, I miss home, but not the damn snow. When he finished he picked up the tray, emptied it and stored it. From force of habit, he slid the chair back in place and arranged the salt and sugar jars on the table. Near the door he moved aside to allow a group of women to pass. His attention was caught by a young slender woman wearing a green blouse. She appeared to have been crying; her eyes were red and swollen. Poor thing, Albert thought, she's probably had a fight with her boyfriend. He turned down the corridor toward his office, eager for the day to begin.

"Good morning, Mr. Garciya."

"Good morning, Mrs. Harris."

"Miss Harris."

". . . fine day, isn't it?"

"Yes. I hope it remains this way."

"Oh! I didn't hear any storm warnings."

"That's not what I mean."

Her voice, Albert thought, is like the musical scale. Do re mi. "Here, take a look at this." She handed him a manila folder, shooed him gently into the inner office and closed the door. She then returned to her cubicle from where she was able to see everything that went on.

Miss Harris reminds me of my mother, thought Albert. And of my Aunt Emma, especially when she wears those dark print dresses. Mostly, thought Albert, her swishy dresses and the soft pat-pat of her sensible shoes remind me of another time, another era. He put down his briefcase, opened the venetian blinds (a habit he had recently acquired) and sat on the soft leather chair to scan his mail. He shuffled the numerous envelopes and folders, putting those affixed with a blue dot to his left. These were not urgent. He turned his attention to a folder affixed with a label on which was written: Monica Rubio. This was affixed with a red dot, the code used by Miss Harris for urgent. He reached for the intercom and in his pleasant voice said, "Miss Harris?"

"Yes?" The brittle voice at the other end sounded unusually cheery. "What may I do for you?"

"I have a folder here with a red dot and . . ."

"I gave you that folder, sir!"

"Uhhh. Yes. Well, can you tell me something about it?"

"Why sir, you're the expert." *Click.* Miss Harris hung up the phone.

Albert sat quietly for some time, then leaning his heavy frame forward, spoke softly and firmly into the machine: "Miss Harris. Please come into my office. Now."

In seconds the spare, bustling figure of Miss Harris, two red dots on her cheeks, came through the door. Albert motioned for her to sit down, opened the folder and asked, "Are you familiar with the Monica Rubio case?"

"Well sir, almost everyone is familiar with *that* young lady. She's most attractive, most of the men . . ."

"Can you be more explicit?"

"Well . . ." Miss Harris crossed her thin ankles, pursed her thin lips, adjusted her spectacles and looked at Albert, who moved forward in his chair. The sun rays formed an intricate pattern on the light, nylon carpet as Albert, his wide feet planted firmly, waited.

"Well, Mr. Garciya, it was this way . . ."

"Garcia. GARR SEE A. Got it?"

"Garcia. Well, sir, I hardly know where to begin. You see, the problem is this: Miss Rubio has filed a grievance against the company, . . . Jocko Brothers. She claims she was forced to work while ill and . . ." Miss Harris paused for emphasis, leaned forward and whispered, "She has created a big problem for us."

"Oh?"

"Yes, sir. A big stink!"

"Well, if that's the only problem, then I think I can . . ."

Miss Harris stood, her print dress clinging to her thin, dry legs, turned to the outer door and in her squeaky high voice announced to a startled Albert, "Why that must be her now. She has a nine o'clock appointment with you and . . ."

"This morning?" Albert could feel his face getting red.

"Why, yes. It's noted on your appointments calendar."

Shit! Albert T. Garcia felt sick. I should have checked the damn calendar and skipped the donuts, he mumbled to himself. He sat down once more, loosened his belt, shuffled papers, then looked up to see Miss Harris walk through the door, followed by a young woman wearing a soft, green blouse.

"Miss Rubio?" Albert got slowly to his feet. "Miss Monica Rubio?"

"Yes."

"Please sit down. I'm Mr. Garcia, the new Affirmative Action Officer. Uhhh, I have your folder here, but have not yet read through it. Perhaps you can tell me what the problem is?" Albert sat back and looked at Miss Rubio, his most sincere smile on his round, pleasant face.

"Where shall I begin?"

"Oh? Just feel free to . . ."

"Well, it's kind of personal, I mean . . ."

"Why, nothing can be *that* personal." Albert, on familiar ground, now continued, a ready smile on his lips. "Whatever it is can be discussed, I'm sure. Why don't we begin?"

"Have you read my personnel file? The report from Mr. Blackstone, my supervisor?"

"Mr. Blackstone?"

"Yes. He's my immediate super . . . He wants to fire me. Everyone knows that. Just because I've been absent a few times. Or so he says." Miss Monica Rubio looked away toward the window where the sun, now warm and bright, lit up the room. "I guess I have a bad record," she said, then turned once more to face Albert.

"Hummmm. Is that all?"

"No." Miss Rubio, her thin shoulders moving slightly up and down, finally spoke in a firm voice. "No. He has always disliked me, right from the start. He picks on me all the time. The other girls can do anything they want, but he watches *me*, what I do."

"Do?"

"Who I talk to, how long I take for coffee . . . And how long I stay in the bathroom. All of that."

"I see. And is that the nature of your complaint?"

"Nature?"

"Is this the reason . . . why you filed a grievance against the company?"

"I didn't file it against the company. I filed it against Mr.

Blackstone."

"He *is* the company."

"Oh!"

"What I mean, Miss Rubio is: he represents the company and . . ."

"That creep. Sorry." Miss Monica Rubio, her eyes to the floor, took a deep breath, then continued. "It makes me so mad. I'm one of his best workers. I never make mistakes. All my stuff passes inspection. I never get any rejects . . ."

"Rejects?"

"Defective chips."

"Oh, I see! Please go on."

"As I said. I *am* a good worker. I do the work of three others combined, but he . . . Mr. Blackstone, still picks on me." Miss Rubio sat clutching her purse, pulling at the thin leather straps.

Albert looked at Miss Rubio, at her heart-shaped face, smooth brow, dark eyebrows and warm hazel eyes. She's been crying, he thought, and is scared of losing her job. I'll have to do all I can for her. He sat up and once more began to question her, his voice soft, understanding. "Miss Rubio, tell me . . . in your own words, just what happened."

"Well," Miss Rubio, alert now, adjusted her pants leg and then in a soft, hesitant voice said, "It's so embarrassing . . ."

"Oh!" Albert felt himself blush. *Damn*. It angered him to know that at forty-nine he still turned red when embarrassed. He coughed, placed his hands firmly on the desk and said, "Please continue."

"Well, it began last year, during Christmas, I think. I caught a cold, then the flu. On the day I was to come back I got sick, so stayed out the whole week."

"I see. Your illness was serious then?"

"Well, first it was the flu . . . then you-know-what."

"What?"

"*That*. You know, my monthly."

Oh! Oh yes, of course. *That*. Albert could feel his face turning red again. *Shit*! He took out his crumpled handkerchief, wiped his brow, took a deep breath and in a squeaky high voice said, "Go on." He tried not to stare at the young woman sitting across from him, but he could not help himself. Miss Monica Rubio was tall, well-formed—a bit thin for his taste—with dark hair and a warm-olive complexion. Not all that pretty, Albert decided, except for the intelligent eyes now focused on him. She reminds me of my daughter, Sylvia. She too is tall, and got a raw deal from her former boss. She didn't know how to fight back either.

Miss Rubio, more at ease now, leaned forward and began once more. "Well, I was absent the whole week. Then Mr. Blackstone wanted a letter from the doctor before he would assign me sick leave . . . and that's when the trouble began."

"Trouble?"

"Yes. He insisted I get a checkup. Then he took me to Personnel. They put me on probation. I guess I have been absent too much."

"Have you?"

"Yes. At least once a month."

"Once a . . ."

"You know . . ."

"*That*."

"Yes. Besides that, he . . . Mr. Blackstone, threatened me." Miss Rubio's voice rose, her face pale. "I hate him. He's always staring at me, making fun. He laughs at all the women, all the, uhhhh, Chicanas . . . Hispanic women. He even has nicknames for us. All the guys laugh at his jokes. Mostly I hate how he looks at me . . . you know."

Yes I do know, Albert wanted to answer, but instead he looked away, shuffled papers on his desk and tried not to show his discomfort. His was a woman family. He had been brought up by his mother, grandmother and aunts. He had no brothers or uncles, only sisters and female cousins and maiden aunts. Albert *liked* women. More than this, he respected women. He resented jokes made by his male friends about women "being on the rag." When Sylvia his daughter began to suffer from pre-menstrual cramps and it was suggested she consult a specialist, he had taken time off from work to drive her to the doctor, all the while sharing in her pain and frustration at what was for most women a natural function. Once he had ventured out on a cold, rainy night to buy her a box of "those things," as he referred to sanitary napkins, and while at the checkout counter was embarrassed to run into a neighbor who looked at the purple box and asked, "Having personal problems, Albert?" He thought too of the countless times he had boiled water to make Sylvia cinnamon tea, said to be good for menstrual cramps. He never minded this; it was the right thing to do. Now, as he listened to Miss Monica Rubio, he felt empathy for her . . . and some pity.

". . . anyway, he threatened me, so I talked to the union steward: Pedro, that is Peter Prendez. He told me to try to get along and not make waves. That's about all."

"Ummmm." Albert T. Garcia sat and thought. Careful. I must be very careful. If the union is involved, I have to play by their rules too. He ran his sweaty hands through his hair, retrieved the crumpled handkerchief and directed himself to Miss Rubio. She looks honest, he had to admit, just a hardworking woman with a personal health problem. Like my Sylvia. Nothing I can't handle. I just have to be patient, understanding. As Affirmative Action Officer I must be fair, honest . . . *affirmative*. "Please finish your story, Miss Rubio."

"Well, as I said. He, Mr. Blackstone, didn't believe me, not even when I told him I've always had trouble with . . ."

"Trouble?"

"Yes, you know. *That*."

"Yes. Well, it states here in your personnel file that you

refused to be examined by one of our doctors. Is this true?"

"Sort of."

"Miss Rubio. I want to help you, but . . . can you be more explicit? Uhhhh, just tell me in your own words," Albert finished lamely.

"Well, Mr. Blackstone refused to give me sick leave unless I went to the company doctor, so I finally went, and . . ."

"And?" Albert could hear his stomach gurgling. Damn those jelly donuts, he thought in disgust, they're making me sick.

Miss Rubio now hunched forward, her eyes suddenly alert. In his chair Albert T. Garcia sat quietly thinking. *Dammit*, why doesn't the union settle this? Why didn't some female steward refer this poor woman to a gynecologist? *Dammit anyway*. He adjusted his tie, wiped his steaming brow and looked back at Miss Rubio. "And what did the doctor find? What was his prognosis?"

"His what?"

"Prognosis! His opinion."

"Well, he didn't have one. He told me to first lie down, but I said I only had a cold. That's when he said . . ."

"Yes?"

"He said he would have to examine me."

"But of course! Isn't that company procedure? A doctor must . . ."

"But he wanted to examine me *down there*!"

"Where?"

"You know . . . that!"

"That? Oh, I see. Pardon my ignorance." Albert felt the sweat gather round his new shirt collar. His belt strained against his ample belly. He cleared his throat, and asked, "And what did the doctor find?"

"Nothing. I mean, that's when the trouble began. He said he would have to have a look at my . . . uhhhh." Monica Rubio sat up, clutched at her purse, took a deep breath and blurted out, "But that's not all he said. He said, 'Lie down, my dear. I'm sure it's nothing new for you.' . . . something like that. He leered at me the whole time."

"I see."

"There was no way I was going to let a strange doctor examine me down there. Not after what he said, anyway. But then, he says awful things to other women. When Bertha Gomez thought she had a lump in her breast, he took a long time examining her. She says he really gave her a massage . . . but what could she do? I hate him. He treats all of us Mexicans, all women like dirt. I'll never let him examine me. Never. I need my job but . . ." Miss Monica Rubio, her thin face agitated, suddenly stopped talking, took a deep breath and slumped back against the chair.

"Ahhh. Then you feel Mr. Blackstone wants to fire you because of this? Well! Let me see what I can do. I'll talk to the union steward first, then to the personnel director. Maybe we can send you to your own doctor or . . ."

Albert T. Garcia felt in control now. His round flushed face was once more amiable, his eyes kind and full of sympathy for the young woman in the soft green blouse. "I'll get back to you in a few days, Miss Rubio." He stood, extended his hand, then watched Miss Monica Rubio walk toward the door, her purse swinging at her hip. He stood looking out the window at the sun, now a rosy red. In a corner, the once vibrant corn plant appeared to droop.

Albert paced the floor, his arms clasped behind his back. *What to do*, what to do for this young woman suffering from this dysfunction. He stood in deep concentration, his hands stuffed into his pants pockets. Here it is the 1980s and yet not much has changed. We send men to the moon, but have no cure for the common cold or women's personal problems. We barely recognize they exist! *Dammit*, why is it women don't know how to take care of themselves? They can't even describe their symptoms . . . what they feel. *Damn*! The pat-

pat of Miss Harris' footsteps jolted him from his stupor. She now stood at the door, her bird eyes expectant and said, "Mr. Garcia, I'm going down for coffee. Can I get you anything?" Albert fished in his pocket for change, then handed it to her saying, "See if they have a jelly donut."

Early the next day, precisely at nine, apprehensive Peter Prendez, shop steward for the assembly and microchip processing line, walked the short distance to the administration offices. He had been summoned to meet with the new Affirmative Action Officer. Pedro, as most people called him, was of medium height, well built and captain of the company softball team. He prided himself on three things: his physique, his ability to down a six-pack a day and his way with women. Although engaged to (as he put it) a "sweet, young thing," he still flirted with the numerous young women who worked at Jocko Brothers. He too was curious about the new AA officer, as everyone now called Albert. His predecessor, Mr. Pinkerton, had been difficult to work with. Everyone called him a racist pig who liked to intimidate the workers, especially minorities. Peter knew of the injustices done to workers, but was helpless to do anything other than to appeal several "forced" leaves and terminations. Well, he thought as he walked towards the gleaming buildings, let's see what this guy can do.

"Good morning, Mr. Garcia."

"Glad to meet you, Peter."

"What seems to be the problem?" Peter was all business. He liked to get to the point immediately and return to his job. Although he was allowed time for union activities, he knew he was being watched and was expected to still do his share of work. "I understand this has to do with Monica . . . that is, Miss Rubio."

"Oh, then you know her . . ."

"Everyone does. What with that *bod*, who wouldn't know her . . ."

"I see." Albert cleared his throat. "I see. From the information in her personnel folder, I see she consulted . . . uhhh, talked to you about her grievance. Could you refresh my memory?"

"Well, it's been some time . . ." Peter felt nervous. This guy sure had a good vocabulary. *Shit*, he was probably from Harvard or Yale and would have all kinds of radical ideas about how he, Peter, should do his job. I'll just play it cool, he decided, and say very little. "Well," he began once more, "she . . . Miss Rubio was told to see a doctor and refused. Then she was refused sick leave by Mr. Blackstone and things like that."

"And did she explain why she refused to be examined by . . ."

"Yeah. She said something about the doctor being a 'lecher' or something like that. To be honest with you, I think she just gets hysterical when she's on the rag."

"What?"

"You know, man. All women get that way. They can barely work."

Albert put his hand to his head, trying to block out the image that instantly came to mind of Sylvia and the ruckus with the high school volleyball team. Due to severe menstrual cramps, Sylvia, then about sixteen, had been absent from practice. Once over them—and armed with a note from the doctor—she had returned to practice. Albert had driven her to the gym and then waited for her on the outside bench provided for players . . . and parents. He planned to wait to watch the girls practice. He could hear the girls laughing and talking. Suddenly one voice roared above the others, Coach Fannery's "Dammit, Sylvia, you miss too much practice . . . and make some lousy plays. What is it with you girls, anyway? Every time you're on the . . . on your period you get hysterical. We've lost three games already! Now, *dammit*, straighten out. No more absences, hear?"

Albert was about to interfere when Coach Fannery walked out to the court followed by the girls. As he went by Albert, the coach waved saying, "I think she'll make it. Most of my girls do. We'll just have to practice till we get it, right, Sylvia?"

"Right."

Now here he was having to either defend or condemn a young woman who, despite her good intentions and productivity, was being set up to be either laid off or fired. Albert brushed off imaginary dust from his desk top, biding for time to contain his anger. In a choked voice he finally said, "Please go on Mr. Prendez."

"There's not much else. I told her to forget the grievance. And not be absent anymore. Life's not perfect, you know. She's just too sensitive. She should learn to take a little kidding, you know . . ."

"No I don't. Explain it to me, please."

Peter felt uncomfortable. This was not how he had envisioned this meeting. He *had* looked forward to meeting Mr. Garcia, even of asking him to try out for the team, but now he wanted only to get out of his office.

Peter Prendez, union steward, took a deep breath, flexed his biceps and said, "Mona, I mean Monica, is too sensitive, that's all. She even threatened to complain if the guys didn't quit whistling at her. That's really stupid, I mean, she's really built . . . She should just learn to take it, to get along. I mean, even her boss . . ."

"Mr. Blackstone?"

"Yeah. Even he likes her. I think he asked her out, but Mona . . . Monica hates him. That's why he gets on her case, 'cause she won't cooperate."

"Cooperate?"

"Yeah. Just learn to take it." Peter leaned forward in his best man-to-man manner, confident that Mr. Garcia understood what he meant. After all, he *was* a man. "I mean, what's a little joke now and then. We don't mean no harm. All the other girls like it, why not Mona? Shit, she should feel good that we look at her. I mean, she's too tall for a woman, but them knockers . . . God, it makes my hands itch just to look at them."

Albert stood up abruptly, hitched up his pants and in a tight controlled voice said, "Peter, your mentality . . . uhhh, your attitude is something else. I mean, do you realize you're contributing to sexism, to sexual harassment? You, a shop steward, are . . ."

"Jesus H. Christ. I was just doing my job!" Peter Prendez, his face contorted, sat with his hands on his lap, waiting for the new Affirmative Action officer to wind down.

"No," Albert retorted, "You were not doing your job. You were going along with others. How would *you* like to be made fun of by a bunch of women? What is the purpose? Why can't you treat women as equals . . ."

". . . equals?"

"Yes. Why make fun of what is a biological function. Answer me. Answer me right now!"

Albert felt suddenly tired. The morning that began with such promise was no more. He sat down, made a note on the file, and then, facing Peter once more, in a less angry voice said, "Next time a young woman complains about sexual harassment, or of intimidation, please take it seriously. Write down each incident, then report it to me. I cannot help anyone if we, . . . I, continue to ignore what goes on. Nor do I find it amusing that, as good a worker as Miss Rubio is, should be discussed as a sexual object. Now please excuse me. I have to see the personnel director."

Once alone, Albert dashed to the men's bathroom, splashed cold water on his face, ran his fingers through his hair and then checked his watch. Good. He had time for coffee and a donut, after which he would see Mr. Pinkerton. He looked out the window at the round sun. He then buzzed Miss Harris to instruct her to make an appointment with Pinkerton for after lunch and went out the door into the warm sunshine.

That evening Albert T. Garcia remained in his office long after Miss Harris bid him goodnight. He felt at odds; the afternoon meeting with the personnel director had not gone well, but Albert was not put out by Mr. Pinkerton's attitude. I miss my wife, Albert said aloud, surprised at the emotion he suddenly felt. She would know what I should do about Miss Rubio . . . and how to handle that sexist pig Prendez, and what I should say in the report to that bastard Pinkerton. Sunny has good sense. All women have good intuition: my mother, my grandma, my aunts. God, I sure miss her.

Albert picked up his heavy briefcase, looked around for his topcoat, then remembering he no longer wore one, he locked the door and walked out to the parking lot. Once at home he opened a can of Spaghettios, warmed the food in the micro and sat down to eat. He sat up past midnight to once more review the numerous rules and regulations and the recently negotiated union contract. When his eyes would no longer focus on the printed matter, he undressed, got into his pajamas, secured the doors, turned out the lights and got into bed. Before he dozed off he said his prayers—a habit acquired in parochial school and still a part of his nightly ritual. In a tired, but fervent voice, he prayed: Please God, let me do a good job. Help me to do what is just, fair. Give me the courage to stand up to those bas . . . to others. And please, God, take care of my wife and daughters. Amen.

The Painkillers

The Painkillers

It was the heat that woke her; an intense heat that permeated the small hospital room and caused her to wake up bathed in sweat. Crista turned over gently so as not to pull at the new scar and feel the intense pain of skin pulling against skin. She vaguely remembered asking the night nurse to lower the heat. It must have been the new patient who asked to have the thermostat turned up.

Crista turned over slowly, tugging at the damp blankets, now almost to her neck, then peeled back the bedspread and light blankets until, exhausted from the effort, she laid back on the firm mattress, relieved to feel the light sheet on her warm body. She looked across at the woman asleep in the next bed. She lay with one thin arm across her face, the long black hair spread out on the pillow. Crista sighed, thinking, I hate to wake her, but I've got to turn down the thermostat . . . or we'll both catch a cold in the morning when they make us bathe. She moved to pull the night cord when she heard the nurse making her rounds. Within minutes the nurse came in, switched on the lights, took Crista's blood pressure and gave her various pills to take. The nurse stood by until she took them. Then she asked Crista the inevitable question: "Need any painkillers, Mrs. Torres?"

"No, I don't hurt as much now," Crista answered softly, then added, "I want to get by without too many pills."

"Fine with me." The nurse moved to the next bed, then gently pulled at the blankets. "Mrs. Lopez, I have to take your blood pressure again and . . ."

"I'm cold. It's cold . . ."

"Mrs. Lopez, I must take your temperature and . . ." The nurse moved swiftly, thrusting her hand underneath the pillow. She propped up the patient's head, took her arm, checked both pulse and blood pressure, then handed her the assorted pills.

"Just gimme a painkiller." The voice was weak but insistent.

"My dear Mrs. Lopez, you had painkillers and an injection less than two hours ago. I'm not allowed to give you any more sedation, unless your doctor gives the authorization. You'll just have to get by without . . ."

"*God Dammit.* I wanna painkiller. It hurts. I have lots of pain!" Mary Lou Lopez, now fully awake, sat up slowly, her hand on her lower abdomen, and screamed at the retreating nurse, "Get me a painkiller . . . and turn up the heat. I'm freezing to death."

When the nurse left, Crista lay still, then slowly stretched her legs feeling the familiar tug. If she called the nurse back, it meant they would both face another barrage from the next bed. Maybe if I say nothing she'll fall asleep again, Crista decided . . . then I can ask the nurse to lower the thermostat. She lay back, pulled the thin sheet over her sprawling breasts and thought of how pleasant life would be now that she had undergone a hysterectomy.

The decision to go ahead with the operation had, in the end, been her husband's. Crista had started to hemorrhage in the car, then had lost consciousness. When the doctor finally arrived, Joe had pleaded with him to operate. He had filled the necessary forms, his long fingers shaking, patted her on the cheek and whispered, "I love you," and then he gave her up to the green-clad nurses who whisked Crista off to the operating room.

After surgery, Crista woke to find Joe sitting next to the bed and holding her hand. "It's over," he whispered in her ear. "It's all over now." Crista tried to mouth an answer but could not. She instead let the medication take control of her and she drifted back to sleep. She later awoke in the hospital room. She felt dizzy from the numerous injections given to dull the pain. She moved to stretch her legs, but felt for the first time the pull of the newly cut skin and cried out.

"Hey, do you need a painkiller?" called the woman in the next bed. "Do you want the nurse?"

"Yes, please."

The nurse was efficient; within minutes Crista was once again asleep, but not before she had turned to the woman in the next bed and mumbled, "Thanks for calling the nurse."

The following day Crista ate a light breakfast and slept through most of the morning, still drowsy from the painkillers. She came fully awake, however, when the nurse informed her she would have to get up and walk to the bathroom. The pain that accompanied each movement made her break out in a sweat, but the nurse—who was holding her by the waist—would not let her stop. Once back in her bed, Crista slept, exhausted from the walk. She awoke once, glanced across the room and saw that the woman in the next bed still slept. The breakfast tray say next to her untouched. The slim figure was hardly visible; only the rise and fall of her breathing indicated she was alive. Poor thing, thought Crista, she is probably in a lot of pain. Just then the lunch carts were wheeled in. Crista ate sparingly of the hot meal, then laid back to sleep. In the next bed the woman turned over and groaned aloud, "I need a painkiller. I'm cold, turn up the heat."

Joe arrived promptly at four, just as afternoon visiting began. He handed Crista a bunch of Shasta daisies and a card which he then displayed atop the hospital chest. They sat, holding hands, talking softly, until Joe finally kissed her and said, "I'll go now so you can rest. I'll be back tonight." He looks tired, thought Crista, as she watched the slim figure retreat down the hallway. Tired, but relieved. She got back in bed and slowly flipped through a magazine, fully aware that the curtain separating the two beds was still drawn across. She pressed her hands to her stomach, parted the thin curtains and walked over to the next bed.

"Hello. I'm Crista Torres."

"Uhhhhh. Hi! My name is Mary Lou."

"Did you have an operation?"

"Yeah. A hysterectomy. They took everything out, even my tubes. All they left was the baby carriage." Mary Lou looked up at Crista.

"Now I'm gonna be sterile for life," she concluded as she reached for a cigarette.

"Well, at least we're alive," Crista began, feeling slightly put out. "I figure I'll be healthy now. At least I won't bleed to death every month," she concluded lamely.

"Got any kids?" Mary Lou asked suspiciously, puffing on the cigarette.

"No," answered Crista, plopping down a pillow on a chair. "I've had three miscarriages and two D & C's. I nearly died the last time."

"I have three kids," Mary Lou said matter-of-factly, "all girls."

"How nice!"

"Not really. My husband wanted a boy. He didn't want me to have the operation until I had a boy, but . . ."

"There's nothing wrong with girls, you know." Crista could feel herself blushing. "There's nothing wrong with being a girl."

"Oh yeah?" Mary Lou raised her eyebrows and smirked. "Huh. Well, to him there is. He wouldn't even sign for the operation, not even when I almost bled to death, until my brother Tudi threatened to knock the shit out of him." Mary Lou sat up slowly, reached for her faded robe, pulled out another cigarette and promptly lit it. She leaned back against the pillow, as around her the white smoke rose upwards.

"Well, at least it's over now," Crista began once more.

"What is?"

"The suffering . . . the blood. Now you can get well and take care of your girls." Crista looked at the thin woman sitting on the bed. She looks young, she thought. Too young to have three children. She leaned back in the chair and tried to think of what more to say. Unable to stand the smoke, she excused herself, waddled back to her bed and laid down. She thought of her own life: of Joe, her parents and of her in-laws who had desperately wanted grandchildren. I've ruined all of their hopes and dreams, she thought, fully aware that they would never accept an adopted child. Well, she concluded, it's over now. She turned over carefully, adjusted the hospital bed and was soon asleep. She awoke later to hear loud voices coming from across the room.

"Gimme a painkiller."

"I'm sorry, Mrs. Lopez, you'll have to ask your doctor."

"I need a painkiller, some pills. It really hurts."

"Maybe before bedtime."

As the nurse went out the door, Crista looked across the room, but the curtains that afforded privacy were once more drawn tight.

Towards evening when the dinner carts were wheeled in, Crista was on the phone with Joe who asked if she wanted ice cream. "Yeah, some pistachio," she answered laughingly. They hung up. She smiled happily across the room at Mary Lou and asked, "What's for dinner?"

"Weeds, just rabbit food. The same thing. I hate it."

"Oh well, can your husband bring something from home?"

"Nah. The garage closes late . . . besides, he eats at his mothers, so he can't," finished Mary Lou, picking at the food.

"Well, I'm really hungry. I'll just have to eat this stuff." Crista moved the tray in close and began to eat.

At seven on the dot Joe walked in carrying a small carton of ice cream. He bent to kiss Crista, lifted her chin and asked, "Almost ready to come home? I already cleaned the house up. I even vacuumed the kitchen."

"So? What will I have left to do?" answered Crista, feigning disapproval. "What am *I* gonna do?"

"Just get well for me," Joe answered softly. He sat looking at her until Crista reminded him that the ice cream was melting.

At fifteen to eight Mary Lou's husband walked in. To Crista he too looked young. He wore a thin grey jacket, dark pants and work boots. His eyes were hidden by dark glasses. He nodded briefly at Joe and Crista as he walked over to his wife and pulled the curtain across.

"How are the kids?" Mary Lou asked by way of greeting.

"Okay, I guess. Your mother ain't said nothing."

"You mean you haven't gone to see them?"

"I just got off work. I ain't even had dinner."

Crista tried not to listen, but it was impossible. The voices carried through the thin curtain. She ate the ice cream thinking, so, this is el Johnny, the Western singer Mary Lou eloped with at fifteen! He sure doesn't resemble an entertainer, she thought, only a mechanic. Earlier that week Mary Lou had described him differently, telling Crista of their elopement and of how el Johnny was popular with women, many of whom came to hear him sing on weekends at The Lonely Hearts Club on San Fernando Road. Crista sighed, then grudgingly accepted another serving of pistachio from Joe. When finished, she looked at him and said, "Gee honey, you really are nice."

"I just want you home."

From across the room loud voices could be heard. El Johnny and Mary Lou were arguing. Crista felt embarrassed but said nothing. She continued to talk softly with Joe who during his visits never took his eyes off his wife.

After visiting hours were over and the halls became silent, the curtain still remained drawn. Crista could hear sobs coming from deep within. Mary Lou was crying! Crista lay thinking; do I want to interfere? What can I say? Unable to ignore the cries that now were mere whimpers, Crista pulled on her new pink robe (a gift from Joe), slowly got off the bed and walked across the room.

"Is anything wrong?" she began, tugging at the blanket.

"No." The voice that answered was angry, hostile.

"Mary Lou, is there something wrong?" Crista persisted.

"No. I tell you."

"Well then, why are you crying?"

"It's el Johnny." Mary Lou's voice cracked at his name. "He ain't been to see the kids and my sister called today and said she saw him at the club with a woman. And," she sobbed, "it's all my fault."

"Your fault?"

"Yeah. He's acting this way 'cause I can't give him a kid. A boy. I knew this was gonna happen. It happened to my sister and my cousin Josie. Her husband went out with some *putas* when she was having a kid. The sobs subsided, then continued with increased vigor. "It's all my fault."

Crista stood awkwardly next to the bed, then sat on the nearby chair. She put her hand to Mary Lou's swollen eyes. "Stop crying," she implored, close to tears herself. "Try to sleep so you can get well."

"But I need a painkiller."

"You have to wait until . . ."

"But it hurts."

"I'll get you one," Crista whispered, "I'll get you one." She sat holding Mary Lou's cold hand in her warm, soft palm as outside the blue sky of evening filled with dark clouds.

The next day, filled with morning showers, heat treatments and the daily walk up and down the hallway, passed swiftly. Crista felt good; the pain was almost gone. That night Joe visited once more. When he left he told Crista, "Two more days and I get you back." He had combed her hair during his visit, his thin finger plying the brush between the strands of hair. He whispered, "I'm no good without you, honey."

After Joe left, Crista read a while. She tried not to notice the drawn curtains. El Johnny had not been to visit. She creamed her face, brushed her teeth and was about to turn off the light, when she heard sobs coming from across the room. She grabbed her robe, tugged at the belt and walked on bare feet across the room.

"What's wrong, Mary Lou?" she began, hoping not to further upset Mary Lou who lay against the pillow, her face a blotchy red, her dark eyes swollen tight.

"It's el Johnny," she said, wiping her nose and reaching for a cigarette, "he didn't come to see me and . . ."

"He's probably working late," Crista said, stroking her hand, "I'm sure it's nothing."

"Nah. It's Friday night and he's already gone to the club." Once more Mary Lou's eyes filled with tears. "He likes it there," she continued, "it makes him feel like he's back in Texas, in Tapi's Club where he got started. He loves the women that hang around . . . and all that. Sometimes," she continued in a stronger voice, "sometimes I wish we had stayed in Texas . . . that way he could sing all the time. But he wanted a steady job . . . and there was nothing in El Paso. Sometimes," the sobs began once again, "I think he's gonna run off with another woman and leave me with the girls. Anyway," the voice grew weary, "it's all my fault. Now he really has a good reason to . . ."

"What reason is that?" Crista asked in a puzzled voice. "What do you mean?"

"I mean that I'm no good for nothing anymore, that's what." Mary Lou's voice rose shrill and loud. "What good is a woman who can't have no kids?"

"But you have three," Crista hissed, "you have three. I'm the one who should be crying." Crista could hear the pain in her voice. "What I mean," she said, "is you can be happy without kids. That's what Joe says." She stood, feeling suddenly tired, and groped her way to her bed. It will be good to be home, she thought adjusting the covers. Our house is nice and the neighbors are good. She lay back trying to sleep, aware of the sporadic sobs coming from the next bed. Crista tossed and turned. The sobs had increased. Oh, what's the use, she finally concluded, all I can do is help alleviate her pain. She reached over, gave a tug to the night cord, then waited for the nurse.

"Give me two painkillers, nurse. I'm really hurting." Crista waited until the nurse left, then quietly walked over to Mary Lou and handed her a pill and glass of water. She waited while Mary Lou gulped down the pill. She pulled the curtain open, secured it, then climbed onto her own bed. Once snuggled down under the covers, she wolfed down the second pill and lay back to await blessed sleep.

The next morning when returning from the shower Crista entered the room to find Mary Lou on the phone. She sounded angry, upset, much like the night before. Embarrassed at having to witness another tearful bout, Crista started to leave, but just then Mary Lou, on the verge of hysteria, plunked down the phone screaming, "*Goddamit*, Johnny ain't paid the rent. The landlord wants to kick us out."

"Oh my God!"

"He wants us out by the first!"

"But that's next week," shrieked Crista. She quickly wound a towel around her damp hair and sat down in the accustomed chair.

Mary Lou sat on the edge of the bed, her thin legs dangling toward the floor. In her hand she held a crumpled telephone book and a pencil stub. Her face was a pale, sickly white. Dark shadows ringed her sad eyes, her mouth was set in a tight, thin line. As she sat scribbling, tears streamed down her face and onto the thin robe.

"*Shit*. Now what are we going to do?" she demanded of Crista. "What are we gonna do?"

Crista moved closer, searching her mind for the right words. She put a hand on Mary Lou's arm and whispered,

"Try calling that pastor. The one that was here yesterday."

"*The hallelujah*?" Mary Lou's eyes opened wide. "You think he can help me?"

"He said to call if you needed anything," Crista said. "Call him."

The day before the jovial and chubby pastor assigned to the Spanish-speaking patients in the hospital had visited their ward. When he came into their room and had introduced himself Mary Lou instantly said, "I'm Catholic," and turned away, leaving him to Crista who, embarrassed and ill at ease, talked with him for a time. When he asked if he could pray over her, Crista hesitated, knowing full well that Mary Lou was watching, then said, "Yes, please." When the pastor was about to leave, he handed Crista and Mary Lou a card. "I have a small Apostolic parish nearby," he said. "If there is anything I can do for you, please call." The minute he was out the door Mary Lou threw the card into the wastebasket, saying, "I don't want anything to do with them hallelujahs." Crista took her card and slipped it between the pages of her address book. She now retrieved the card, handed it to Mary Lou and said, "Here. Call him."

Once back in her bed, Crista laid back on the rumpled sheets to try to nap. Now and then she looked across at Mary Lou, frantically dialing and talking on the telephone. Tomorrow I'll be home, she thought, home with Joe. She glanced out the window at the grey sky and then back to Mary Lou who was still on the phone. She dozed off and on until the dinner trays came and went, while Mary Lou continued to dial and redial. When Joe came, they talked quietly. He admonished her to be ready at nine. "I'll be here early," he said, looking down at his hands. "I want you home." Crista said nothing, too happy to speak.

The last night Crista lay in her hospital bed, waiting for the painkiller to take effect. Already she felt drowsy. She glanced across the room at Mary Lou who was now sound asleep. The numerous phone calls had depleted her of what little energy remained. The dinner tray remained untouched; el Johnny had not been to visit. It *was* Saturday night. Fun night at the Lonely Hearts Club!

When Joe left, Crista had complained to the night nurse about the increasing pain. She was given two painkillers. Once again she gave a pill to Mary Lou who wolfed it down and quickly fell asleep.

I hope the pills don't kill her, thought Crista, suddenly contrite. But they sure worked last night. It's all I can give her, she rationalized, it's all I can do to alleviate her pain. Maybe Joe will take me to hear el Johnny. She smiled at the thought of Joe in a club, then drifted off to sleep.

In her narrow bed Mary Lou lay half asleep. She could feel the painkiller working in her system. She took a deep breath and once more laid back to await the sleep that would release her from the stigma of being sterile, from the pain of having a wandering husband and the thought of how different her life might have been if she had only given birth to a boy.

Adios, Barbarita

Adios, Barbarita

I am on my way to see Barbarita. She is leaving for Mexico this morning, never to return. She made this arrangement with my father; when he died she would return to Mexico to live. We recently buried my father. And now she is leaving. I will not see her again.

I am to drive her to the airport. Everyone else is busy, or so they say. The truth is Barbarita has not been too kind to our family. There is much hate and anger towards her, much of it justified. But I have none. I have come to love Barbarita. You see, she is all I have of my father.

When I first met Barbarita she called me *la mas chiquita*, the smallest one, although I was a married adult with children. I'm not sure if she was trying to win me over, but I recall being pleased by her words. My father too appeared pleased. Since that day, now almost thirty years past, I do not recall hating Barbarita nor ever exchanging harsh words with her. But the others did. The truth is Barbarita caused dissension in our family, but I remember other things.

I remember how Barbarita cared for my father. When twice he underwent surgery at an advanced age she remained constantly at his side. Although I had young children and did not work outside the home, I did not feel obligated to have to care for my recuperating father. He had Barbarita to clean, cook and care for him.

I often visited my father and stepmother alone. My noisy children upset Barbarita, but this did not bother me. I enjoyed these private times when Barbarita told me of her life prior to meeting my father, a sixty-year-old widower. Barbarita often described her favorite movie stars and celebrities seen on *el canal* 34. Many afternoons we sat in the dim living room talking softly as nearby my father dozed full of food cooked by Barbarita, secure in her care.

Barbarita liked Chinese food. Often I visited in late afternoon once the children were home from school and I had found a sitter. First I would dash to Mings Kitchen, buy three dinners (complete with cookies) then drive at top speed hoping to arrive while the food was hot. Oftentimes my father did not want *las hierbas*, as he called Chop Suey, so Barbarita and I ate all three dinners including the fortune cookies, which I first would translate. It made me happy to see Barbarita gorge on sweet and sour pork. For long I had seen her toil at a hot stove, even on hot, steamy days, cooking *cocido*, my father's favorite dish.

Barbarita was good to my father. She served him breakfast promptly at eight, a full course dinner at noon and a light supper at six. I often felt I owed her so much for the care she gave my father. Now and then I brought pistachio ice cream. It became her favorite.

I'm ready to leave but first I must make a stop at Mings Kitchen. I want to surprise Barbarita with stuffed eggrolls, a dish she especially likes. I wait impatiently for the waitress who finally hands me a white carton. I dash to the car, put it in gear, then take off.

The freeway is crowded; I fear I will be late and Barbarita will miss her flight. I pull away from slow cars, then fly down the fast lane to Barbarita.

After my father had died I visited Barbarita, but it was not the same. She now greeted me with a curt *buenas tardes*. She felt I too was anxious to be rid of her. But I did not feel this way and once tried to assure her, but she did not believe me. I felt her cold, suspicious glance . . . and quickly looked away. I don't think Barbarita hates me, or anyone else, only her circumstances: that of an elderly widow in a strange country whose language she never conquered.

When first I heard that Barbarita was going home to Mexico I felt terribly sad. I would no longer be able to talk to her of my father, of his ways, sayings, fetishes. I liked to hear Barbarita discuss my father, although not everything she said was complimentary. But you see, I know the truth when I hear it, so when she slipped up and said things a daughter should not hear, I listened . . . I believed her. And although these were mostly small, petty things, I know it is small, petty things that sometimes drive women crazy, so I sympathized . . . and continued to visit. And now she is leaving and taking memories of my father with her. And I am beginning to cry.

I don't want Barbarita to leave. More than once I have told her: there is no reason for you to go. *Para que se va?* Why are you going? Her answer was: *Aqui no tengo a nadien. Nadien, nadien.* I have nobody here. You have me, I want to say but hold back. It is clear she does not want me.

I am near the house. The family home was sold soon after my father's death, as he instructed. Barbarita is awaiting legal papers and her portion of the house sale that will enable her to live in Mexico. I do not begrudge her this money. She more than earned it.

When last I saw Barbarita she appeared weak, her voice a low whisper. When I inquired after her health, she gave me a cold, hard look and said, "Crees que yo tambien me voy a morir? Do you think I'm going to die too?" I was shocked. I did not answer. We then talked of inconsequential things: the weather, the soaps and Mexican movie stars. Now and then she looked off into space, her brooding eyes ringed with dark circles. As I was about to leave she informed me this would be our last visit. She wished to sever all ties with our family. I stood, not knowing what to do when she closed the door in my face.

The following week I learned Barbarita had obtained her passport, bought new luggage. Several times I picked up the phone to call. When she did not answer I was relieved. And then one day she called. Would I drive her to the airport . . .

out of respect for my father? Yes, I responded, wanting to add: out of respect for you! But after giving me the date and time, Barbarita quickly hung up.

I am almost there. The eggrolls, nestled in the antiseptic white carton are tempting. I am hungry. Very hungry. I did not have time for breakfast, what with having to send the children to school and put the house in order. But I don't dare pick at the food. I want it for Barbarita. I want her to see that I care.

I am at the door. Barbarita, dressed in a black dress that hangs to her ankles, is waiting. It is hot outdoors; she will probably roast in that outfit, but I remain silent. Perhaps it is appropriate that she is dressed in black. Barbarita hands me the suitcase at her feet, which I put in the car trunk, and a garment bag that looks fairly new. I want to compliment her on such good taste, but the last time I commented on a new sweater she took offense and inferred I was curious as to how she spent my father's money. So I say nothing while I lay the bag carefully in the back seat where it will not crumple.

It is time to leave. I reach into the front seat, remove the food cartons and with a smile hand them to Barbarita. She asks what it is, beginning to frown. "Did I tell you to bring me food?" She says in Spanish. "No, no," I stammer, my face suddenly hot. "It's a surprise." She tells me to eat it myself, she doesn't want it.

I remain standing, the cartons in my hand, not knowing what to do. Barbarita picks up her purse, locks the door, then walks to the car. She wants to arrive on time, she says in a tired voice.

I adjust my seat belt, put the food on the floormat. Once she is seated, I move it next to me. Somehow its presence consoles me.

I drive. Next to me Barbarita sits quietly, her wrinkled brown hands clutch her purse. Cars whiz by. I turn on the radio hoping to find a Spanish station, but then remember

Barbarita prefers television to radio. She appears impatient, moves around in her seat. I pick up speed. I had hoped that once more we could talk of my father, laugh at something silly he once said or did, but her silence silences me. I drive on, humming softly to myself.

I enter the parking lot, buy a ticket, find a space, then remove Barbarita's bags. I hand them to a porter (or whatever they call them at the airport), then follow her inside where she is processed and given a boarding pass. We ride the escalator to gate 20: Aeronaves de Mexico. Her step is firm, steady. I appear to lag behind.

I ask if she wants coffee, wanting to prolong her departure. No.

Her flight is called. She is leaving after all! I feel the tears start. Shit, I'm going to babble all over the place. I turn away, but she has seen me.

"Ay criatura! Apoco estas llorando?" she asks in disgust. "You are not crying?" "Si," I mumble, averting my eyes.

"Don't waste your tears on me," she hisses, her dark eyes searching mine. "After all, I was nothing to you all."

"But to my father . . ."

"Si, but he's gone," she states firmly.

They are boarding. I want to hug her, but she moves with the line. She is leaving. I will not see her again! Adios, Barbarita, I call. Adios. She does not hear me, or pretends not to. She does not look back. The stewardess checks her pass; I remain by the door, my eyes glued to the slight black figure that disappears around the bend.

The plane is warming up. I hear the roar of the engines. I move aside to allow a late passenger to enter, then stand near the window. Adios, Barbarita, I sob quietly. Adios, señora. I wish you had stayed. I would have visited you. I would have taken you to church, to the cemetery, the movies, dinner. I would have!

She is leaving! Barbarita is leaving. She is taking my father with her. She is taking his memory with her. I am going to pieces . . . and she is going to Mexico where she will probably die as will memories of him.

She is gone. The silver airplane is no longer visible. She is gone. I walk to the parking lot. I feel drained, empty. I have done my duty.

I am inside the car. The tears come fast, hard. I lean on the steering wheel, not sure of whom I cry for. For Barbarita, who in her old age is returning to a country she once disdained? For my father? For myself?

I cry all the way to the freeway. I miss hitting two cars. I turn the radio on full blast and cry along with the English group Yes:

Owner of a lonely heart
Owner of a broken heart

I accelerate, pass other cars. Now and then I hum along; now and then I cry. I am home. I park the car, reach for my purse and spot the food containers. The Chinese food bought for Barbarita is still in the car! I open a container. I take out a mushy egg roll. I sit quietly thinking of Barbarita and of my father, as I munch on an eggroll . . . salted by the tears that run freely down my face.

The Permanent

The Permanent

Altagracia Diaz rose early, as was her custom. *Siempre madrugadora*, her mother had teased her when as a child she was the first to get up each morning. She walked to the bedroom window, opened the shutter wide, then stood on bare feet to breathe the cool mountain air. This is the best time of day, she thought. The whole day before me, *for* me. Her slight body, outlined by the flannel nightgown that flapped around the ankles, was tall. Her white hair stuck out from a well-shaped head. Her eyes, like two black peas, darted here and there: to the lock on the fence, to the birdhouse (now empty of visitors) and to the sage covered mountains behind her house. Altagracia—or grace, as she was now called—enjoyed inspecting her domain, as she referred to the small clapboard house and the yard with neat rows of onions, tomatoes, and cilantro, and most of all, her pride and joy: the stately rananculas she nourished each Spring. The back yard was left bare for her old dog, Peter Thomas, to hide and dig up bones and stay away from the flowers. Altagracia thought back to the first time she saw this house and her happiness at seeing the walnut trees that dominated the large yard. They reminded her of the family home near Camarillo. These trees were the main reason she and her now-deceased husband had bought it. On this quiet morning the walnut leaves covered the ground. Daily, she collected and saved the fragrant grey-green leaves. Once dry, they made a soothing, tasty tea.

Altagracia wound her arms around herself to ward off the morning cold. She stuck her bare feet underneath the braided rug made from scraps of material, remnants left over from numerous dresses, curtains and cushions made in the years before her vision had failed. Altagracia thought back to the many winters spent in the maple rocker next to the television set she seldom watched, where she would cut the material into strips. As she went into the kitchen, the sun was already reflecting on the warm, glossy leaves.

In the small, spotless kitchen, Altagracia plugged in the coffee percolator that she had filled the night before, she selected a piece of pan dulce (the kind without sugar) from beneath the glass cake holder, and then sat down at the dining table. As she ate, she thought of how peaceful her life was, of the silent house no longer overrun with children, dogs, noise. When finished, she looked at the wall clock out of force of habit, rinsed the cup, spoon and saucer, dried each piece and replaced them in the cupboard, walked into her bedroom and began to make the bed.

Earlier that year she had retired from Thomm Aircraft Company after 35 years as an assembler. She had vowed to take it easy, relax and do less housework, yet found that each morning she still hurried to make the solitary bed immediately after breakfast. She went outside to check on Peter Thomas. She saw that all was well, and went back into the quiet house.

Today was Saturday, the magic day when extra chores, shopping and errands were done, and phone calls were made to friends prior to a Sunday visit. On this day trees were watered, rocks moved, weeds eliminated. White sheets that were hung on the clothesline during the week were brought down, inspected for rips, then folded into a perfect square and put to rest inside the chest at the foot of her bed. On Saturday too, floors were scrubbed the old fashioned way: *con garras*, with the rags that she kept under the sink. Yes, thought Altagracia, Saturday was a day to get things done and to pamper herself a bit by having her hair styled.

When the complimentary ticket for a free wash and set arrived in the mail, Altagracia called the Joy of Life Beauty Shop and made an appointment. She took pride in how she looked, or as she said, "on how I present myself." She disdained women who let themselves go to "pot." Her hair was kept short, neat, as were her nails. An apron was never worn twice. She often laughed at what women of her generation, the 1940s, considered the ultimate compliment: "You can eat off her floors." Ha, she thought, those days are long gone. Anyone who dares to eat off my floors today will probably get sick.

Altagracia hurriedly finished her bath then rechecked the house and Peter Thomas and then left for the beauty shop. She planned to use the 10% discount ticket for senior citizens, but was embarrassed to have her friends know this. She hated the idea of handouts, welfare, *la ayuda*. She called this her stubborn Mexican pride, but knew it was mostly the Anglo notion that all minorities were on welfare, out for a "dole." This repulsive idea was one shared by many of her former co-workers and had been the source of many heated arguments. She locked the house, got into her compact car and sped off.

Altagracia arrived at the beauty salon to find it half empty, except for two young women sitting under dryers. Her white hair was shampooed and set in rollers. After that she settled down to read *People Magazine*. She was visibly relaxed, in a daze from the intense heat of the dryer, when the shop door burst open. In walked a heavy-set Mexican man holding a small child in his arms, while another clung to his leg. He was followed by a slender young girl and a slim older woman. Altagracia took one glance at the group, then brought the magazine up to her face.

The man wore a clean white shirt, buttoned at the collar and tucked into dark cotton pants. Across his ample waistline rode a hand tooled leather belt with a shiny buckle that read, "*Tome* Coors." His wide feet were encased in cowboy boots with thick heels and pointed toes. He held a wide-brimmed cowboy hat; a red, white and green flag peeped out from the hat band. His clean-shaved face was round, the eyes a steady brown, the nose short and flat. Gold rimmed teeth glittered in a wide smile. He approached the desk and said, "Uhh, Mees, Mees."

"Yes? May I help you?"

The man stood, feet spread wide, hat in hand, the smaller child stradling his wide arm. He motioned to the girl to stand next to him. "Anda, Marisela, dile a la señorita que queremos." He gently shoved the child that clung to his pants leg, shifted the baby to his other arm, all the while smiling at the slender woman, apparently his wife, who smiled back.

The woman appeared to be in her early thirties. She wore a blue cotton dress with short sleeves. The small, finely chiseled face was framed by straggly hair that was held in place with a green rubber band. The light caramel-colored eyes darted here and there, as if frightened. In one hand she held a brown plastic diaper bag containing a baby bottle and a box of Pampers. She clutched her purse while eyeing the other women in the shop who were sitting securely underneath hair dryers. She turned to her husband, her light eyes beseeching. Once more the man spoke to the young girl, "Anda, Marisela. Dile a la señorita lo que . . ."

"Ahhh, Miss," the girl moved to the desk. "Miss, my mother she wants *un peinado*. Uh, she wants her hair to be fix-ed."

"Why of course! Tell her to come this way and I'll begin on her." As she spoke the beautician's blond curly hair bobbed up and down. The bright blue eyes were kind as she added, "Tell your mother to sit here."

"Mama, dice la señora que te sientes. Alli." The woman sat where the girl indicated, then quickly pulled her dress down over her knees. Just then the younger child, the boy that clung to the man's legs, began to whimper: "Papa, Papa, quiero hacer chi." From beneath the dryer Altagracia sat, cringing at the sight.

My God, she mumbled to herself, why can't they go anywhere without twenty kids? Why can't they learn English? She thought back to when her children were young. She had taught them to wait quietly when inside stores. Never had she allowed them to run around, especially inside a beauty shop. Altagracia tried not to look at the woman in the nearby chair who sat with a nervous, expectant look on her face, as water dripped off her hair onto a towel.

"And just how do you want your hair styled, Miss?" asked the beauty operator as she untangled the wet hair with a clean comb. "Just how do you want to look?"

"Uhhh. Pos, uhhhh . . ."

"Oh! You don't speak English? Well, that's okay dear. I'll find someone to interpret for you." The beautician looked around the room. Her eyes narrowed on Altagracia who looked down at her magazine and turned the pages slowly, thinking, *Not me. Not this time.* She turned the pages for a time, aware that others were looking her way. She brought the book up to her face.

"Tell you what," the operator motioned to the girl, "you tell me, okay? Have your mother tell me how she wants her hair."

The young girl moved forward, eager to be of service. Her light eyes, similar to those of her mother, shifted from the beautician to her mother to her father. Her eyebrows, like small, black wings, met in the middle; her pug nose sniffed at the air. She wore faded blue jeans and a pink tee-shirt. The word HI was written across the front. In her hand she clutched a brown leather purse with stenciled pink flowers. The small pink mouth smiled at everyone.

"Marisela, dile a la señorita lo de tu mama," ordered the man.

"Si, papa." The girl took a deep breath. "Uhh, Miss. My mother she wants a . . . mama, dice la señorita que como quieres el peinado?"

"Ahh. Pos asi. Asi como ella," responded the mother.

"Entonces le digo? . . ."

"Sí."

"Oh. And what does she want?" asked the beautician smiling broadly. "Ask her how she wants to look."

The girl slowly turned, looked directly at the operator and in a clear voice said, "Miss. She says she wants to look like you." The light eyes remained steady as she repeated, "She wants to look just like you."

"Oh my! Is that so? Well, we'll see what we can do. She'll have to have it cut and styled. Can you tell her that?"

"Yes. Mama, dice la señorita que ahorita te va a peinar."

From the doorway the man smiled his approval. Inside the shop the younger boy began to spread magazines around the clean, shiny floor. Suddenly the boy began to clutch at his pants and whine, "Papa, quiero hacer chi."

Good God, thought Altagracia, suddenly angry. Why doesn't he just leave and take his brat with him? Just then the man walked toward his wife, his heavy boots leaving behind a pattern of black, oily marks. In a booming voice that appeared to fill the room he said, "Bueno, vieja. Me voy pa' que el chavo haga chi." He then pointed to the girls saying, "Y tu, Marisela, no dejes sola a tu mama." He turned, started for the door, the small boy clinging to his pants leg, the baby snug in his arms. Just then the boy threw himself on the floor and began to screech, "Papa, Papa, quiero un dulce."

Suddenly the man turned from the half-opened door to yank at the boy as he hissed, "¿Pero, no es que querias hacer chi?"

"Un dulce papa. Quiero un dulce." With that, the boy pulled away, threw himself at his mother and with renewed vigor began to scream "Quiero un dulce."

From her chair Altagracia glared at them. *Good God, viejo gordo, niño chipil. Why don't you just leave*? Once more she touched her hair, dismayed to find it still wet, and brought the magazine to her flushed face. The man grabbed the screaming child, pushed open the door and walked out of the beauty shop. With a timid smile the young girl walked towards Altagracia, picked up the magazines on the floor and laid them neatly atop the stack. Altagracia did not look up.

When she first saw the operator lead the woman toward her, Altagracia cringed in her seat. God, I hope she sits somewhere else, she mumbled. However, the only available seat was next to her. The operator adjusted the controls, then urged the woman to sit down next to her. Altagracia tried to concentrate on the magazine article. She could feel the woman's gaze, but refused to acknowledge her. *Not today, not this time*, she thought. Just then the door opened; the child who had cried earlier entered at a run, jumped into his mother's lap and began to jump up and down.

Altagracia felt the hot anger seeping through her, as next to her the slender woman wrestled with the young boy. When forced to the floor by his flustered mother his foot hit Altagracia on the knee. "Sientese." The word was out before Altagracia knew it. She felt herself blushing, but no one appeared to have heard her. The boy looked at her with childlike curiosity and then, unperturbed, moved to sit near the door. Once more the young girl rearranged the magazines. Still Altagracia did not look up. Suddenly the blonde operator appeared, brush in hand, and walked to the woman, put a hand to her head and said, "Ahh, almost dry? Good. Follow me. We'll comb you out, yes?"

"Jess."

The woman, her dark head covered in a bright pink net, moved from beneath the hot dryer, smiling at everyone as she moved across the room to be combed out. Through the shop window her husband could be seen pacing back and forth on the sidewalk. In his arms, the small child, now pacified by a milk bottle, slept. Behind him walked the older boy, a popsicle dangling from his mouth.

Inside the Joy of Life Beauty Shop the curly haired operator began to untangle her client's shiny mass of curls. She sprayed, teased and twirled the hair, then stood back, smiled her approval and handed the woman a mirror. The slender woman slowly got out of the chair, smiled at her image and beckoned to her husband.

"You're going to be so happy," gushed the smiling beautician, her face warm and friendly. "Uhhhh, you know. Happy?"

"Si. I know appy."

Just then the heavy-set man, trailed by the young boy, walked in, handed the sleeping baby to his wife, opened up his wallet and said, "Ha muchi?"

"Well, let's see." The operator scribbled on a notepad as she enumerated: "Shampoo, set. Uh, ten dollars."

"Papa. Dice la señorita que . . ."

"Ya se. Esto, si, se entiende." The man handed the operator a bill and in a gruff voice said, "Anden. Vamonos."

They exited the shop as they had entered: in a tight, close group, the man in the lead, followed by the older boy now munching on a candy bar. The young girl walked behind her mother, the warm eyes riveted on the curls that bounced up and down. They crossed the street, climbed into the pickup and sped away. From her chair Altagracia breathed a sigh of relief audible to the other women, all of whom burst out laughing.

"God, did you see the stomach on him?"

"And all that gold!"

"Well, they sure learn fast. About beauty shops, I mean."

"Yeah. All except English."

Altagracia sat quietly, her small eyes glittered dangerously, her mouth twitched in anger. Unable to control herself, she turned to the laughing women and in a hoarse voice said: "I heard what you said."

"Oh yeah?"

"Yeah. And I want you to know something. I'm Mexican too and . . ."

"Yeah? So why didn't you help them?

"Well, what I mean is my kids never behaved liked that and . . ." She never finished. Just then a pickup truck pulled over to the curb, brakes screeching. It was *them*! They were back. All eyes were on the door as it opened with a bang.

The Mexican man, visibly agitated, stomped into the beauty shop, followed by his frightened daughter. His wife and the younger children remained in the truck. He walked straight to the reception desk where the blond beautician stood. He was visibly angry, his Texas hat crushed in his hands. His boots clanged on the floor as he bore down on the operator that minutes before had worked on his wife.

"Mees," he began. "Uhhh, mees." Then he turned to the young girl and said, "Marisela, dile a la señora que . . ."

The girl turned to the blond operator and in a faltering voice said, "Miss, my father, he wants to know what you did to my mother."

"What I did? Tell him I did what you told me!"

"What I told?" the girl frowned, then glanced at her father.

"I asked what you wanted and you . . ."

"Ahhhh."

". . . you said she wanted a hairdo just like mine!"

The girl stepped back, turned to her father and in a small voice said, "Papa, dice la mujer, . . . la señorita, que el peinado de mi mama es lo que ella queria." She stopped, then looked across the room at Altagracia. "Papa, ¿que le digo?" she pleaded.

"Dile que tu mama queria un permanente. *Un permanente.*" His voice was loud and clear. Around the shop women looked up, startled at the disturbance.

"Miss," the girl valiantly began, "my father says my mother she wanted *un permanente.*"

"A permanent? But you said she wanted to look like me!"

"Don't you have a permanent?"

"No, dear. I have very curly hair."

The girl stood still, her hand over her mouth, her eyes opened wide. The beautician, her eyes beseeching, her voice contrite, spoke directly to the man. "Señor, I'm terribly sorry. Comprende? Sorry. Sorr-ee."

"Si. Yo se de sorry."

"I can do her hair over. For free. I'll give her a *permanente* if you bring her back. Uhhh, next Saturday?"

"Si."

The man pocketed the refund, turned and walked out the door. The young girl, happy at the results of what she had feared would be an unfriendly argument, smiled across the room at Altagracia. Once more they walked out toward the pickup truck. The young girl climbed into the truck bed, then held out her arms for the young boy. She waved farewell at the beautician who stood at the door, blonde curls bobbing. Once more she looked toward Altagracia, who averted her glance.

From the safety of her chair Altagracia sighed with relief. She felt suddenly tired, worn. The day had not turned out as planned. She felt both guilty and angry. She sat, unaware of the voices in the small, hot room, trying to sort out her mixed emotions, then got up, threw the magazine on the stack, ran her fingers through her now dry hair, walked to the cashier, plunked down a ten dollar bill and walked off.

"Just a minute, Grace," called out the receptionist. "It's only five with the coupon."

"I don't need the coupon."

"But . . ."

"I can afford it. Not all of us need a handout." Altagracia walked out the door to her car.

Once at home Altagracia parked her car, opened the gate for Peter Thomas, then let herself into the quiet house. Her anger was spent. But she felt guilty. Very guilty. She walked to the calendar, made a mark directly beneath the next Saturday, then stood looking out at the walnut trees. I will go to the beauty shop next Saturday, she vowed, and this time I will be of help. I will no longer impose my value system on other Mexicanos. I will not think of them as different, as *them*, but as us. And, I will be of some help. With that, she settled down on the maple rocker for her afternoon nap, and was soon asleep.